HIS PAIN MY GAIN

VOLUME IV

TRANSFORMING

POWER OF THE

BLOOD

PASTOR DON R. VINING

ISBN 978-1-969865-54-1 (Paperback)
ISBN 978-1-969865-55-8 (Ebook)

Inquiries and Book Orders should be addressed to:

Leavitt Peak Press
17901 Pioneer Blvd Ste L #298, Artesia, California 90701
Phone #: 2092191548

DEDICATION

This book is dedicated to all who have found, and will find, Christ as Lord and Savior. Thank you for allowing me the privilege of teaching the message His Pain, My Gain. It has been proven, time and time again, that the more we learn about the sacrifice our Lord and Savior made for mankind, the stronger our lives become, enabling us to live the higher life in Him.

ACKNOWLEDGEMENTS

My thanks to Connie Neumann for another job well done in taking hundreds of pages of notes and capturing the message of His Pain, My Gain.

My highest gratitude to Brenda Ammons for her many hours of research and typing on this project. Without her dedication, this project would only be a dream, instead of a reality.

My appreciation to Suzi Scott, Glynda Roberts, and Kay Green for proofreading.

My heartfelt thanks to Dr. Carol Bartholomew for another outstanding cover design that flows with the subject of this project.

CONTENTS

INTRODUCTION

In their song, "Everything to Me," the group Avalon says that Christ is more than a story, more than words on a page of history. But is He that in your life today? Or has the reality of Christ's suffering lost its significance in your life?

Too often we think of Christ's suffering as something that happened too long ago to have any effect today, but that is not the case. The prophet Isaiah said, "with his stripes we are healed" (Isaiah 53:5).

Christ bled a total of seven times before His death, beginning with His agonized prayer over us in Gethsemane. With each distinct time He bled, He confronted and conquered every trial, situation and circumstance that we have faced, or ever will face, in our lives. Because of His suffering, we are covered by His blood. And that blood is powerful.

We do not have to be slaves to the past or to our current situations, because Christ suffered for us. By gaining a true understanding of what His suffering meant, of its eternal significance, we can move into deeper fellowship with Him.

Do you want to step boldly out in faith? Do you seek freedom from bondage? Then use His Pain, My Gain as a tool to further your spiritual walk and to take your Christian life to the next level.

Truly, His pain has become my gain. Without His blood, we are lost. But because of it, we can live free, victorious lives for Him.

Pastor Don R. Vining
Belleview FL.

1

CHRIST'S SUBMISSION TO THE FATHER

I am amazed at how many believers live their lives in Christ without ever really understanding the depth of Christ's sufferings. Through these sufferings, Christ literally covered every issue or circumstance that would ever dare touch our lives. When He suffered, He suffered for our total freedom. Just as our veterans fought for the freedom of our country, so it was with Christ.

If we truly understood the significance of Christ's suffering and the way He agonized over the sin of this world, we would never dare to sin again. Do you have trouble with sin every now and then? According to the Bible, we all fight sin because no one is perfect: "There is none righteous, no, not one" (Romans 3:10).

As I learn more about the sufferings of my Lord and Savior, I become a better person, a stronger person. It is my desire to become the light of the world that Jesus has com missioned me to be. Every measure of Christ's suffering has a very significant meaning for our lives. His suffering was more than just dying. He literally bled seven times to fulfill the will of His Father concerning our lives.

Start With the Shroud

First, let's discuss the shroud in which Jesus was buried. The garment that was found with stains on it is believed to be the one in which Christ was wrapped and buried. Understanding that Christ

1

was now dead on the cross, a man came and asked if he could have the body of Christ for burial. The biblical account describes the scene in Luke 23:52-53 this way:

> *This [man] went unto Pilate, and begged the body of Jesus. And he took it down, and wrapped it in linen, and laid it in a sepulchre that was hewn in stone, wherein never man before was lain.*

In his book A Doctor at Calvary, Dr. Pierre Barbet wrote that in the year 436, the Empress Pulcheria had the basilica of St. Mary of the Blachernac built in Constantinople. There she deposited the burial linen of Jesus:

> Now the shroud is a linen burial cloth about 43 inches broad by 14 and ½ feet in length. Scientists and archeologists have both tried to prove as well as dis prove whether or not the shroud that was found was the actual one that Christ was buried in. The piece of garment that was found was a piece of tissue of pure linen, close and opaque, made of course thread of which the fiber is unbleached. The material most certainly belonged to the age in which Jesus lived. All the images that were present on the shroud are the result of a simple impregnation of the threads, an impregnation which would have been facilitated by the fact that linen is an excellent absorbent material (A Doctor at Calvary, Pierre Barbet, MD).

To give you an example of the nature of this type of cloth: years ago, I decided to show up at a particular party as a mummy, so I had my wife wrap me in gauze from head to toe. Then I said, "Now cut my mouth out." And that she did-her scissors clamped down on my lip! As I was gurgling "Urrh…urrh," blood began to pour. I can tell you this type of linen definitely stains with blood. If you have never had scissors applied to your lips, don't try it at home.

The images of the wounds on the shroud were quite a different color from the rest of the body because of dried blood, which had sunk into the material. The strongest images were at the side. When the garment was originally discovered, its finders could only see with the natural eye. The stains-later proven to be bloodstains were strongest at the side, the head, the hands and the feet. Remember, Jesus' side was pierced.

Scientists submitted the shroud to many strange tests in order to prove its authenticity. According to Dr. Barbet, it was boiled in oil and also washed, but the markings were impossible to remove. Do you know what that tells me? What Jesus did, no man can alter. The price He paid with His own blood can never be washed away. Hymn writer Robert Lowry wrote, "What can wash away my sin? Nothing but the blood of Jesus."

Why Christ?

Some accept that a corpse must have lain in that shroud, but question whether it was Christ's body or that of some other man. This body bore all the stigma of the passion, meaning that this body bore all the markings of the crucified Christ. Other men were crucified, but to our knowledge, our Lord and Savior was the only one crowned with thorns. Also, there is nothing to explain how the corpse left the tomb. Removal of the body would have destroyed the shape and the markings of the linen. The linen was lying there. Something had obviously once been wrapped in it, but now there was nothing there. If someone had touched that cloth, it would have been out of shape and out of place. In fact, the Word tells us in Luke 24:12 that Peter arose and ran to the tomb, stooped down, and saw the linen cloths laying by themselves. He left wondering what had happened.

The good news is that we don't have to wonder any more. By faith and by what the medical field has proven, we know Christ lived, died, and rose again from the dead. We're not serving a dead

Christ-we are serving a risen Savior. Jesus Christ was beaten, bruised, and gave His life.

The story is real. The blood Christ shed was shed for you and me. The bloodstains that can't be removed are from the same blood that has power to remove sin from our lives. I thank God that the blood of Jesus is real. I thank God that someone was bold enough to test the linen to prove, once and for all, that it could only have been the body of Jesus wrapped in those linen cloths. We no longer have to wonder if the resurrection is real. It is real! Jesus is real. His life and his blood and His forgiving power are real.

We serve a risen Savior. We don't have to worship a plant or an idol, but can worship the risen Christ. That is the reason we don't bow down to Buddha, but we stand up and say, "Thank You, Jesus, thank You, Jesus; thank You, Jesus" for the blood is real. You've heard the old saying, "the proof is in the pudding." For Christians, the proof is in the linen.

The Trail of Blood

Next, let's look at this trail of blood. Christ bled for us seven times, but we often think He only bled on the cross. However, through a deeper understanding of His trail of blood, we can see that His blood covers our Christian walk every step of the way. Luke 18:31-33 says:

> *Then he took unto him the twelve, and said unto them, Behold, we go up to Jerusalem, and all things that are written by the prophets concerning the Son of man shall be accomplished. For he shall be delivered unto the Gentiles, and shall be mocked, and spitefully entreated, and spitted on: And they shall scourge him, and put him to death: and the third day he shall rise again.*

You may be walking through trials and tribulations, but the third day is coming. You may feel deader than four o'clock and poorer than a house cat, but let me tell you, the third day is coming. Through this trail of blood, each step and each drop reveals a deeper level of power in our spiritual journey.

The pure and spotless Lamb of God met the profound will of His Father at the gates of Gethsemane. Luke 22:39-43 tells us:

> *And he came out, and went, as he was wont, to the mount of Olives, and his disciples also followed him. And when he was at the place, he said unto them, Pray that ye enter not into temptation. And he was with drawn from them about a stone's cast, and kneeled down, and prayed, Saying, Father, if thou be willing, remove this cup from me: nevertheless not my will, but thine, be done. And there appeared an angel unto him from heaven, strengthening him.*

When you are down and weak in your spirit, the Lord is going to send an angel (Psalm 91:10-12). It doesn't matter if you are suffering in your body: there's an angel on the way. It doesn't matter if you are financially distraught: there's an angel on the way, and that angel is carrying and representing the blood of Jesus Christ.

Even if you've already prayed for that husband, or wife, or child, keep on doing what you've been doing, because there is an angel on the way. If the Lord God Jehovah sent an angel for His own Son, how much more will He send an angel for you and me?

Luke says this about Jesus: "And being in an agony he prayed more earnestly" (Luke 22:44). That means when things did not feel right, He got down to sincere business. I've had people say, "Pastor, I have been praying for a long time, but I just can't get through in my prayer life." Have you agonized? Have you really set your heart and mind to it? One Sunday morning, someone stopped me and said, "Pastor, today I need my miracle. Not next Sunday, not a year from now, not next week, but today,"

Have you agonized to the place that you've become sincere in your walk with Christ? The Scriptures tell us that when Christ was in agony, "He prayed more earnestly." This is the first time Christ bled for us. Verse 44b says, "and, His sweat was as it were great drops of blood falling to the ground."

According to the Biblical Illustrator, "The Mount of Olives reminds us of the Savior's pity on those who perish. Those tears fell from eyes that had looked into eternity and knew the work of souls." He knew that we were worth nothing, doomed for a devil's hell if He did not shed His blood for us. He agonized over what He was seeing in the spirit. "The Mount of Olives is identified with the supplication and intercession of Emmanuel and so suggests to us the Lord Jesus as the great example in prayer" (Biblical Illustrator).

I believe with all my heart that the shroud is that of Jesus. Secondly, I believe that on the Mount of Olives, Jesus gave us an example of how we should submit ourselves in prayer.

> In praying for His people, the Mediator's prayer was absolute. He said, Father, I will. But, in praying for Himself, how altered was the language: Father, if it be possible, let this cup pass from me. Nevertheless, not as I will, Lord, but as Thy will (Luke 22:42). He not only submitted Himself in prayer but there was perseverance in His prayer (*Biblical Illustrator*).

In other words, Jesus prayed until He got an answer. I believe we need to do the same thing. People tell me, "Well, Pastor, I pray every now and then." You should pray every day until you get an answer. When you leave your home, you ought to be praying. While you are studying, you ought to be praying. While you are listening to the doctor's report, you should be praying. While you are looking at the bank account and wondering why it is in the red for the nine teenth month in a row, you should be praying. While you are talking about that vehicle that won't half run, you should be praying and seeking God: Lord, I want to bombard heaven until I get through to You.

There are stories from the old-time Pentecostal movement of people who so desperately wanted the baptism of the Holy Spirit upon their life that they packed a suitcase, brought it to the House of the Lord, and said, "Preacher, I'm not going home until God fills me with the Holy Ghost." Imagine what would happen in the House of God now with that kind of perseverance, if people would say, "God, I'm not leaving here until I get my miracle. Lord, I've been depressed, confused, and frustrated. The devil's been chasing me, and I've been wondering what my life is supposed to be all about-but, Lord, today is the day. Forget the races. Forget football. Forget dinner. I'm not leaving Your house, Lord, until I persevere. I believe this Word, and I'm not leaving until I become a spectacle of this Word."

I've seen enough to know that if Christ prayed, I need to pray. What would happen if the people of God came together in unity and said they weren't leaving until they were changed? We need to ask the Lord to take out the old heart and put in the new. We need to pray until He takes the addiction away so we can come and lay it on the altar. We need to pray until we can lay the credit card on the altar. Christ, our example, knew how to pray.

Preparing For Trials

The best preparation for trials is habitual prayer. Whether you feel there is a trial on the way, or you are already in one, the best antidote is to get on your face before God. You see, long before Gethsemane became the scene of His agony, it had been the Savior's private chapel. "The Mount of Olives recalls us to the Savior's affection for His own. The love of Jesus is little credited, even by those who have some faith in His finished work" (*Biblical Illustrator*).

For several reasons, Jesus commenced His sacred passion, or deep internal love for mankind, in the garden. First of all, He intended to follow His usual custom. After He had preached and wrought miracles, it was His practice to take Himself away to pray. Let me tell you, preachers and teachers of the gospel are most susceptible to attacks of the enemy five minutes after God has used them through His anointing. Why? Because then they are mentally and physically drained. Jesus knew that after He had wrought miracles, it was imperative that He retire to His private chapel and pray to the Father before He went to sleep.

I want to encourage you, parents and grandparents, in the battles you have been fighting. When you have done all that you can do and have allowed God to use you, it is imperative that, before you sleep, you get on your face and pray, "Lord, thank You for helping me through another day."

When I get through preaching, I find a private place and say, "Lord, thank You for letting the Word flow one more time. And, God, if anything was accomplished; it was You who accomplished it." I tell Him that I know who I am. I am nothing except that the blood of Jesus Christ saved me. If our Lord and Savior cried out to His Father, surely I must cry out as well.

Jesus Meets Us Where We Are

One of the other reasons Christ went to the garden is that, as the second Adam, He would make satisfaction in the Garden of Gethsemane for the sin of the first Adam, which had been committed in the Garden of Eden. That tells me that no matter where I am, Jesus is coming to me. Jesus went to the garden because sin had its day in the Garden of Eden.

Whatever garden you sinned in, hold on, because Jesus is coming. And when He gets there, the power of His blood is going to flow over that place. This is why the Bible says that when we ask forgiveness of sin, He not only forgives, but He forgets those sins. Hebrews 8:12 says, "For I will be merciful to their unrighteousness, and their sins and their iniquities will I remember no more."

Have you ever tried to read through blood? Prick your finger and bloody up a piece of paper, and then try to read through it. You can't do it. If you can't read through your own blood, how much more the blood of Jesus covers the sin of mankind.

Wherever you are suffering, wherever you are in bondage, wherever you are hurting, wherever your turmoil is, whatever is going on in your home, Jesus is at the house waiting for you. When you get there, you are going to find that the power of the blood of Jesus has washed away the sins of your home. Jesus always goes to the place where the enemy has attacked His own. He comes to my place of torment; He comes to my place of suffering.

His Stripes For Our Healing

By His blood and by His stripes, we are healed. What does it take for that to happen? Like Abraham, all we have to do is believe. Say, "Lord, I believe You died and rose again, and I believe in the power of Your blood. I believe that I have eternal hope in Jesus Christ because of the blood You shed for me. Thank You, Lord, that I don't have to come running to You, but You are running to me today."

Knowing what lay ahead of Him, Jesus realized-perhaps for the first time all the agony He was about to go through so He could be a "sin bearer." He had to bear the sin of the world.

When He stood where we should have stood and paid, to His Father's justice, the debt due from us, He paid what He did not owe. It was the sin of man, not the sin of God. But Jesus stepped in and said He would pay for the sin of mankind, because man does not have the power to give his life. Man could never be the perfect, blameless sacrifice, but Jesus could. Jesus knew the price He would have to pay, but He still said He would go to the cross for us. That is why Jesus came.

Before He gave His life, He went to the garden and sweat began to pour like great drops of blood. Medically, that is impossible. Think about it. It was this that laid Him low-the sin of the world. To be treated as a sinner, to be smitten as a sinner though in Him was no sin. This is what caused His agony. Trouble of spirit is worse than pain of body:

> Pain may bring trouble and may be the inciden-
> tal cause of sorrow, but if the mind is perfectly
> untroubled, how well a man can bear pain. When
> the soul is exhilarated and lifted up with inward
> joy, pain of the body is almost forgotten (*Biblical
> Illustrator*).

Not long ago, I was speaking with a man on the phone and he told me he had a migraine headache. I began to thank him for his calls and his ministry, and before long he said, "Do you know what? My headache is gone." Do you know why? Because the mind was no longer troubled.

Jesus did not have a physical problem. He agonized over what He was about to go through for us. It was the soul conquering the body. On the other hand, the soul's sorrow will create bodily pain. The Savior's bloody sweat was caused by an inward struggle. He was seized by fear and horror of His passion and death, but at the same time, He was burning with zeal for the honor of God and the redemption of man. He sweat blood in the strictest sense of the word-natural blood, in a natural way. He was sorrowful; He fell upon His face.

Luke talks about Jesus' sweat becoming as drops of blood trickling down upon the ground. According to the *Biblical Illustrator*, the Greek word here is *thrombos*, which means "clot." This has always presented translators with difficulty, because they say that clots cannot come out of the body. However, Dr. Barbet says,

> This happens with an intense dilation of capillaries under the skin, when capillaries under the skin come in contact with sweat glands which are distributed over the whole skin and they burst. The blood mingles with the sweat and it is this mixture that pearls over the whole surface of the body.

Think of being in such agony that the body not only produces sweat, but produces blood clots. Christ agonized to the point where His internal body was in such disarray that blood began to mix with sweat and it began to clot. Can you just imagine the pain of a clot coming through the skin?

A friend once took me fishing and we caught several cat-fish. I grabbed a fish as he was going to get the hook out of its mouth, and one little barb sunk down in my hand. It didn't hurt so bad going in, but when I tried to pull it out, guess what? You talk about a grown man crying. It hurt. I can only imagine the pain of blood clots popping through the skin.

> Once they reach the outside, the body coagulates with the clots, which are thus formed on the skin. They fall down on the ground being forced by the profuse sweat. Though there is an enormous fall and vital resistance after such a hemorrhage, this would be a very serious one (*A Doctor at Calvary*, Pierre Barbet, MD).

We usually think nothing really happened to Jesus until they crowned Him with thorns and drove the nails into His hands and feet. But long before He got to that place, He agonized over us. If you do not know Him as Lord and Savior, He has been agonizing over you for a long time. Long before the cross, He cried to the Father over you. He has gone to the Father countless times and said, "We must shed grace and mercy upon that soul. One day he is going to walk the aisle. One day she is going to fall on her face,"

If "part-time" Christians could understand what price Christ paid-even before the cross-they'd never again say, "I didn't go to church because I didn't want to." And never again would someone call the preacher and ask, "Can I put my tithe money toward a trip to the beach?"

Long before I ever felt God in my life, He was agonizing over me. My mother went through a whole lot before she delivered me nine months later. Take the agony of a mother and multiply it by the sin of the world, and you get a taste of what Jesus walked through. He fell on His face and cried out to the Father, not only for fear of what He was going to face, but because He knew if He didn't walk through this horrible death time, you and I would have no hope.

The Father's Will

The Father wants to work His will in your life. His will cannot be present in your life until you accept Him as Lord and Savior.

Christ submitted His will to the Father when He said, "Not my will, but thine, be done" (Luke 22:42). That also what happens when you accept Him as Lord and Savior. At salvation you are saying, "I commit my purpose over to Your purpose. I commit my will over to Your will."

We can't really celebrate Easter until we understand the price Christ paid for us. Technology has proven that the shroud is real. We have proven by the inspiration of the Spirit that He prayed and agonized over us to the place that He bled. That's why the Bible says, "So shall my word be that goeth forth out of my mouth: it shall not return unto me void, but it shall accomplish that which I please, and it shall prosper in the thing whereto I sent it" (Isaiah" 55:11). Because of what Christ did before, the cross was not void. By committing His will over to the Father, He became an intercessor for us.

Do you know how to tell when someone's really in this "God thing"? Because everything changes from "me and my will" to "Lord, what would You have me do?" Every time you ask, He will lay on your heart someone to agonize, pray for, and cry over.

There are people who need a touch of God Almighty on their life. In fact, they've listened to people tell them all their lives that they are nothing. But, while the world, their mama and daddy, brothers and sisters, family and friends have been telling them that they are nothing, Jesus was agonizing over them. What He did at Gethsemane, He is still doing today. He still agonizes over your life. He loves you. Thank God, He loves me when Momma and Daddy walk out on me. When brother and sister curse me, Jesus loves me. When the church gets up and walks out the door on this old boy, thank God, He loves me.

He is always agonizing over me, about the things that are to come. I don't know what's going to happen next week, but this week He is agonizing. Great drops of blood are pouring from the head of Jesus. He sits at the right hand of the Father, and I believe He is saying, "Now, Father, You know what the boy is going to go through next week. But We are going to go ahead and cover him with the blood."

Every Step of the Way

From the moment you accept Jesus and commit your will to the Father, the blood of Jesus covers every step you take. You can walk, like Jesus did, into a devil's hell, but it doesn't matter. What can man do unto you? What can the devil do unto you? He can do nothing. What can cancer do? It can do nothing. What can a heart condition do? It can do nothing. What can a divorce do? It can do nothing. Why? Because you are covered by the blood of Jesus! To those of you who are retired, you need to know that Jesus is still agonizing over you to accept Him as Lord and Savior.

Wherever you are, Jesus is coming to stand by your side. In fact, by His Spirit, He is with you now. No matter what life has dealt you, you can stand, you can be bold, and you can be an overcomer. You can make it in Jesus' name because of the blood of Jesus. No matter where I go, or what I walk through, the blood covers me. No matter who comes against me, or how much money I do or don't have, I am covered. Thank God, the blood covers me.

O saint of God-why is it that you live a life of fear and agony when He became agony for us? Why do we suffer and pay a price He already paid for us? It is time we understood that long before He got to the cross, He agonized.

Thank God, there is hope for someone like me. I've been told my entire life that I was nothing. I was told I could not have a wife or children, and that I was eaten up with leukemia and would die. I would never make it as a businessman, I was told, and they sure enough told me I could not pastor a church. But they did not understand who had been agonizing over this old boy.

You want the fear to be gone? Then understand it was Jesus who paid a price for your life. Jesus Christ and Him crucified. It took me a long time to understand that Jesus is my source. He is my Redeemer, my hope, and my power. Jesus is the one I trust-not the community, not the building, not the bank, not Mom and Dad, nobody. I have been delivered from the sin of man, and, thanks to God, I am covered by the blood of Jesus.

When someone says, "How are you doing?" I say, "I'm covered!" Jesus gave His life that I would have life. If I am Baptist or Presbyterian, black or white, Jew or Gentile, I'm covered. If I've accepted Christ's finished work on Calvary, I am covered.

When the devil comes up this week to tempt me, I will say, "Devil, I am covered!" How many times has the devil sold us the religious lie that if we're not Baptist or Presbyterian, Methodist, Catholic, Church of Christ, Church of God, Assembly-whatever-we're going to hell? Here's the bottom line. The only way you will have the damnation of hell is if you refuse to accept the One who agonized over you. I love my church and I love my family, but they are not my salvation. It is the One who agonized. People told my daddy, "You should have shot him years ago." He said, "Yeah, I reckon I should have." But, thankfully, he didn't; today I have purpose, because the blood of Jesus covers me.

You say, "I'm hurting." Yeah, but you're covered. "But I'm suffering." Oh, but you're covered. "I just don't know what I'm going to do." You're covered-so hold on. Hold on. Even when you don't know what to do, stand firm. Stand in the knowledge and the wisdom of His Word. Be like Job, who vowed, "Though he slay me, yet will I trust in him" (Job 13:15). No matter what I feel in my body, I know in my heart I am covered.

Still Agonizing

Jesus agonized in prayer over us then, and He's still doing it today. "Oh, but Pastor, now that I am saved, He doesn't agonize over me." No! No! No! No! Until He hears me stand before the Father, and the Father says, "Well done, thou good and faithful servant" (Matthew 25:21), He'll keep agonizing over me. Wait a minute. Am I saying that after you've been a saint for forty years, you still have a Christ who agonizes? Oh, yes! Christ won't quit on you.

Let me tell you a little faith-builder about the blood. Sister Betty Lanier, in Cleveland, Tennessee, had a brain tumor and asked our church to pray for her. We prayed for months that God would heal her and cause that tumor to be gone. She was supposed to have brain surgery, but the doctor decided to wait several months before he operated… She wrote our church a letter recently and said, "Pastor, thank you for your prayers. I went back to the doctor this week and he says there is no swelling in my brain. I can do anything I want to do."

We're covered. No matter what you are going through, don't give up on your faith or your hope, because Jesus started bleeding a long time before you even came into the picture. It is the blood of Jesus that will heal your troubled, sinful soul. To every person hurting, struggling, and dealing with trouble in life, let me say again-it is Jesus you need. It is Jesus who bled and died for you. For every person who is seemingly without hope, He is your hope.

One of the things God is doing in these days is tearing down denominational barriers. Christians of every walk of life are beginning to understand that we serve the same God. Are you living and trusting in Him now? Do you understand that no matter what lies ahead, you are already covered? These days, when people tell me I am nothing, I just smile, because they don't know what I know. Long before the cross of Calvary, I was covered. Let them mock me all they want, because when they are hurting and in need, they are going to come running to the truth. "And ye shall know the truth, and the truth shall make you free" (John 8:32).

No matter what your background-if you are hurting, struggling, or in bondage; if you are wondering what you are going to do with your life, understand that Christ loved you so much that He gave His life so you might be covered with His blood. The "religious spirit" says, "Well, I've already prayed." I'll tell you the truth. I'm going to pray until I get through. If you are struggling, know that Jesus is your answer.

Thank You, Lord, that in the Garden of Gethsemane, as great drops of blood in the form of sweat rolled off Your face and body, You were agonizing over the sin of the world. Help us this day to live like we believe that. And give us the courage to give an answer to everyone who asks a reason for the hope that is in us (read 1 Peter 3:15b).

Praise God, we are covered by the blood of Christ.

2

NOT ONCE, BUT
SEVEN TIMES

When we look at the reality of Christ's suffering, most of us shut off mentally, because we've heard it so many times before. We think, okay, Christ was nailed to the cross, He bled, they placed Him in a tomb, and He rose on the third day-that's it. But the real issue is that Christ bled seven different times, not only on His way to the cross, but at and on the cross. Have you ever gone through a problem and wondered, "Has God dealt with this before?" I submit to you that the Lord has dealt with and conquered every-thing that has and ever will touch your life.

> The blood of Jesus is the primary theme that the Holy Spirit has for the church today. All power which flows to mankind with redeeming grace and glory flows because of the blood of Jesus. No confusion about the Savior's person or His work can abide in an atmosphere where the blood and the cross are taught in the light of God's Word (*Biblical Illustrator*).

You may have a confused mind, but in the name of Jesus, by the blood of Jesus, the confusion can't stay. I've heard people say, "Pastor, I've been confused about my miracle." In the name of Jesus, confusion has to get up and walk out. Our God is not the author of fear and confusion. He is a God of understanding. The gospel is easy to understand. When it becomes difficult, it is because man has made it such.

In the name of the Lord God Jehovah, there is no confusion that can stay in your house. No power of hell can withstand the proclamation of the blood of Jesus, whether it is declared from a pulpit, or spoken over a home or a heart. In fact, on the cross Jesus said these words "It is finished!" (John 19:30.) In the same way, I believe whatever it is you are going through, Jesus said, "It is finished." The devil thinks he has you on the run and thinks he's about to wear you out. He doesn't understand that the Word, through the blood, is about to wear him out.

I read the end of the Book, and it tells me I don't lose, I win. I may be sick in my body, but through the blood of Christ, I am well in Jesus' name. I may be confused in my mind, but because of the blood, I am healed in Jesus' name. I may be worrying and wondering what tomorrow is going to be like, but because of the blood, my mind is settled.

If you believe that the blood has covered you, you ought to stand to your feet and say, "Lord, I thank You that I am covered. I thank You that confusion can't stay. I thank You, Lord, that I've been redeemed by the blood of Jesus!" Thank God it doesn't matter what denomination we've been raised in it's the blood that makes the difference. Just look at the devil and say, "You may as well let me go, because by the blood of Jesus, I have been set free. I am whole in the name of Jesus." No power of the enemy can withstand the power we have through the blood of Jesus Christ.

Start at the Root

It was no accident that the first time Jesus bled was in the Garden of Gethsemane, because sin started in the garden. Jesus will always go to your point of attack. Here's the reason we cannot conquer certain issues in our lives: We want to pick up where we think we should, but God says we must go to the root of the problem. You're going to find that the root of the problem, the real issue, is that we have a false belief about the way we are supposed to be healed. People tell me they just don't feel healed. That's part of the problem we shouldn't worry about what we feel. We should, by faith, thank God that the doctors figured out what was wrong so we can pray specifically. "Lord, I know that You bled and died for this disease and, thanks be to God, I'm healed in Jesus' name. Disease, hold on all you want to, but in the end you're gonna dry up and fall off, for I have been made whole in the name of Jesus."

In the Garden of Gethsemane, Jesus agonized as He turned His will over to the Father. Turning our will over to the Father is a difficult thing it isn't something you do on a Sunday morning and that's it. You make a decision to be saved. Then you need the rest of your life to learn how to be set free of what you were saved from.

People stutter, "But I prayed the prayer 30 years ago, and I'm saved." Often what we say and how we act are two different things. If we are truly saved, foul words should never be heard out of our mouths, and foul actions should never be observed from us; only Christ, and Him crucified, should be seen living through a sanctified vessel.

We make a decision to be saved, but through this life, we are being saved all day long. The once-saved-always-saved belief is taught in many places, but if I'm covered for life, why do I have to repent every day? The Apostle Paul speaks of dying daily in 1 Corinthians 15. This simply means we have to repent every day of things we have done. Every day of our lives, we have a responsibility to commune with the Lord and say, "Lord, now I've learned my lesson from yesterday. What is it You want me to learn today?"

For example, Saul had an encounter with God on the road to Damascus. According to the Scriptures, his name was changed from Saul to Paul. If you read the history of Paul, you will find that for more than three years after his conversion, no one heard anything from him (cf. Galatians 1:18). During this time he was learning more about the God he had chosen to serve. The next time you read about Paul, his message was so powerful the religious leaders wanted to take his life (Acts 9:23). According to James 2:20, "faith without works is dead"-meaning we are saved all the day long by living the Word.

I believe we suffer affliction (sickness) in our bodies because the Lord is trying to teach us how to trust Him. If you have an illness, are you closer to the Lord today than you were before you found disease in your body? Do you feel more loved by the Lord now than you have ever felt before? I believe that's the reason the Lord allows disease to come. It isn't that the enemy is running rampant to take you out. God is allowing this in your life to show you that no matter what the devil brings, God is greater. And it's all because of the blood.

Just as Christ became an intercessor for us in the Garden of Gethsemane, when we turn our will over to the Father, we are covered by the blood. When we make intercessory prayer for someone else, the blood covers us. When you lift loved ones up in prayer, you don't even have to pray, "Cover them with the blood," because it is already done. Christ bled for them that they might be covered. People say they've been covering themselves for years. No. By faith you pray to be covered, but it is the Lord Himself who covers you. It was the shedding of His blood, not your blood.

Christ's Scourging

The second time that the spotless Lamb of God bled for us was when He stood accused of breaking the traditions of the law. The appropriate penalty for this was scourging. Mark 15:15 reads, "And so Pilate, willing to content the people, released Barabbas unto them, and delivered Jesus, when he had scourged him, to be crucified."

The instrument of torture used upon Jesus was the cat-o'-nine tails whip. "The whip was made up of leather plats. Into the plats were woven iron spikes or balls of lead or knuckle-bones of animals that were located at some distance from the end" (Biblical Illustrator). Before Christ was scourged, He was stripped of His clothing before the people. That alone would have been humiliating enough. Then His hands were bound above His head, and attached to a marble pillar. With Him bound this way, the blows from the whip were even more catastrophic.

The thongs would cut the skin, and the balls and bones would dig deep into the bruised wounds. The outer skin was stripped-in other words, the dermis, which is the skin below the epidermis, would lie open. They beat Jesus until skin and meat were literally ripped from the muscle. If you have ever skinned an animal, you can well imagine what happened to Jesus. There would have been a great deal of hemorrhaging, and vital signs would have dropped dangerously. Therefore, Hebrew Law limited the number of strokes to forty. "But the Pharisees, who were precise people wishing to make sure that this number was not exceeded, had reduced the quantity to 39" (Biblical Illustrator).

The Significance of 39

This number is significant. It is reported that there are actually 39 major illnesses in the world today. Christ was beaten 39 times-one for every illness represented. That tells me if there is cancer in my body, He was beaten for me. That tells me if I have AIDS-even though it's a major, life-threatening disease-He took a stripe for me. That tells me if I have leukemia in my body, if I have colon cancer, breast cancer, a brain tumor, or some other disease, Christ had me on His mind. At any moment He could have said, "That's it. I'm not going to suffer anymore." Instead, He said," nevertheless not as I will, but as thou wilt" (Matthew 26:39). He took the beating for us, His children, knowing we'd be headed to a devil's hell full of sin and disease if He didn't pay that price.

Whatever you struggle with, fear not. You have been covered by the blood of Jesus Christ. It was important to the Lord to heal you. Read and research the Word, and you will realize Christ spent three years upon this earth healing the sick, but only six hours giving His life for the sin of the world. This is not to minimize or make light of His suffering in any way, for it was very significant. The three years of His healing ministry on the earth were a prerequisite to the ultimate sacrifice-six hours of intense suffering and then the ultimate giving of His life. We count the three years leading up to His death as insignificant, but Christ spent those years walking about the earth, teaching, and healing the sick. He even raised the dead. Christ has a sincere interest in your being healed of each and every infirmity.

In Luke 8:49-56, we read about a little girl that everyone thought was dead; when the Master showed up on the scene, however, He removed all doubters from the room, and the little girl was brought back to life. Let confusion and doubt be gone in the name of Jesus. When the Master walks into the room, if we praise, acknowledge, and magnify Him, then He can do the work He came to do.

To me, Christ's three-year healing ministry demonstrates how really, desperately important it was to Jesus that you be healed. That's why the Word says, "With his stripes we are healed" (Isaiah 53:5). Whenever I speak on this topic, people tell me it's easy for me to say, but they've not had that experience. Even when you don't feel it in your body, let your faith go to work and say, "Lord, I'm not living by the doctor's report, but by Your stripes I am healed."

Thirty-three years ago, a doctor told my parents that their six-year-old boy was going to die of leukemia, but I live today because they believed in the risen Savior and the stripes that He bore. Long before this boy needed salvation, he needed to know the Healer.

Mastering the Flesh

Through His suffering, Jesus also shows us the flesh is to be mastered by the Spirit. He not only heals us, but He has given us the power to overcome our problems. I don't have to be beaten with a cat-o'-nine tails. Thank God, I don't have to be nailed to a cross. All I have is to be willing to say, "Lord, as I live this life, no matter what it deals me, no matter what circumstance, or who or what comes against me, praise God, I'm healed."

Folks sometimes ask what they should do when they see cancer and problems in the church. Long before the miracle, stand up and begin to proclaim that by His stripes, the ministry is healed.

If the world ever needed a message, they need to know that by the stripes of Jesus, we are healed in His holy name. We are covered by His blood. We are covered by His grace and mercy. We are covered by His power and by His Word.

Accusations of Blasphemy

The third time Jesus was beaten and bled for us was when He was accused of being the King of the Jews and the Son of God. They accused Him of being a blasphemer and crowned Him with a crown of thorns. Mark 15:17-20 says:

> *And they clothed him with purple, and platted a crown of thorns, and put it about his head, And began to salute him, Hail, King of the Jews! And they smote him on the head with a reed, and did spit upon him, and bowing their knees worshipped him. And when they had mocked him, they took off the purple from him, and put his own clothes on him, and led him out to crucify him.*

The crown itself was not just a headband, but a sort of cap made of thorny branches. Scholars believe the thorns were very long and sharp, and came from a thorn-bearing tree. "Such a crown would have wounded the surface of the cranium and also the forehead" (Barbet). Think about it.

According to Mark 15:19, the crown was driven against His head by blows with a reed-a stick. Now, the best example that I could give you is if I were to take a concrete block and begin to scrape it with a steel chisel. Eventually, the block would turn to powder. It is the same torment as with the crown of thorns. Every time someone hit Christ, or when He pulled Himself up to breathe while on the cross, the crown of thorns dug into His skull. Mankind in human flesh would have never been able to suffer the torment. That kind of pain would make you want to lose your mind. When you feel like that, hold on. He suffered this for you, even as that crown of thorns dug into the mind and the skull, and began to peel away human flesh.

Just like that crown of thorns, the devil comes to steal, kill, and destroy. Hear me, oh precious saints-the devil doesn't want you to hear this message that would cause you to receive your miracle. But if you will receive the truth, you shall be set free in Jesus name.John 8:32 promises that "Ye shall know the truth, and the truth shall make you free" The truth will set you apart from the false. Just like that crown of thorns dug into Christ's head, the devil comes to dig into your head. He whispers, "That husband of yours really isn't what you need. That wife of yours really isn't God's will for you."

Know Your Enemy

In Genesis, when Adam and Eve were in the garden, Adam was out doing whatever Adam was doing, but Eve was there, and the Bible says there was one working: the serpent. He was lurking, roaming to and fro, trying to find a way to get into Eve's head.

The enemy is sneaky. He will never come to you directly and say, "I'm going to put cancer in your body. I'm about to rip your home apart." The enemy is more cunning and worse than a wild beast. When a wild beast comes through the door, you know he is going to tear up the house. But sometimes he comes in as a Jezebel, in sheep's clothing. The spirit of Jezebel isn't always a woman. But the spirit of Jezebel can get on preachers, teachers, and on a good old tithe-paying saint.

Many of you can't receive your miracle because your mind is so distraught. For fifty years, some of you have been taught that healing was for Old Testament times. But I'm going to tell you -you are healed today. Not yesterday, not last month, not in the Old Testament. If He healed in the Old Testament, thank God, He heals in the New Testament. The Old Testament was an account of a nation. The New Testament shows us how to live a holy, righteous, delivered, set-free-and-healed life.

I'm taking this Word literally. I believe Isaiah 53:5. By His stripes, I am healed! I know what it is to feel I have lost my mind, but I also know what it feels like when the Spirit of the Lord comes and says, "Son, everything is going to be okay." At that moment, the mind comes back.

Have you ever been out on the road somewhere and for-gotten where you were going? Not long ago, an uncle of mine called home and asked his wife, "What car did I drive to the store?" He had completely forgotten. When she got there, he was leaning up against his own vehicle and didn't even know it.

There are a lot of you who are leaning up against the words of the enemy. He has come lurking. He has come to mess you up and block your mind. I dare say some of you are sitting there, thinking, "I don't believe He can heal me any more than He can cause me to walk on the moon." I tell you, if He chooses, He ran cause you to walk on the moon.

By His stripes, by the cat-o'-nine tails, by the crown of thorns, He chose to bleed and die an awful death that I might live. That means I'm healed, in Jesus' name, People ask me if my body hurts. Yep, but that's okay it just doesn't understand that it is healed. It's still responding to yesterday, but He paid the price for my agony.

It is time for us to walk in faith. Quit trying to figure it out. Stop trying to know what is right and what is wrong; just give Him praise and honor. When He rose from the dead, His suffering became His glory. And when He comes to the House of the Lord by His Spirit, it is His glory that rests upon you. Anytime you experience His glory, you have to experience His miracle via salvation. "For the Son of man is come to seek and to save that which was lost" (Luke 19:10), "But he was wounded for our transgressions, he was bruised for our iniquities: the chastisement of our peace was upon him; and with his stripes we are healed" (Isaiah 53:5). Say to yourself, "I'm covered in Jesus" name!"

When that devil meets you at the front door and reminds you how bad you feel, say, "Devil, while I'm hurting in my body-did 1 forget to tell you?-1 am covered!" The old lawn mower might not crank, but I'm covered. The old car might have left me on the side of the road, but I am covered. My wife may have walked out on me, but, thank God, I was covered before she got there, and I'm covered now. My home may be broken, but I am covered. And in Jesus' name, my home is coming back together.

The doctor may have told you that your body has contracted an awful disease. But just say, "Doctor, I thank you, I respect you. God has helped you identify the problem so I know how to pray.

I'm going to follow your orders, but at the same time, I'm going to give Him praise and magnify and glorify Him." You'll never receive a miracle unless you first believe.

People tell me they've been taught that when you go into the House of the Lord, you hold your peace. No! The Bible teaches that if we are the children of God, we tell the devil, "Greater is he that is in [me], than he that is in the world" (1 John 4:4). The devil doesn't have dominion over me.

Why do we still struggle? Because we are still trying to work it out. We are still trying to understand that when the ugly report comes, it is only there to teach us how we should pray. When I had leukemia, it wouldn't have done one bit of good for my mother to pray for my big toe to be healed. Here's the common prayer: "Lord, You know that I have a need. Lord, if You will heal me and make me righteous... Lord, if You'll let me win that lottery...." You can pray it and pray it until you draw your last breath on the face of the earth. God already knows. He's already touched by the feelings of your infirmities. He already knows what you need. Then how should we approach Him? How should we pray? Our part is to praise and magnify Him.

The Reason For the Thorns

Jesus was crowned with thorns to mock Him. He bled so that when I stand and proclaim the gospel and people mock me, I'm covered by the blood. You've been cursed, you say. Well, so have I. And it doesn't really feel that bad anymore, just common stuff for me. I'm not going to get sunk by someone's cursing. I'm bigger than that, in Jesus' name. I'm not Peter, but sometimes I feel like I am walking on water. I am covered.

When Christ was in the Garden of Gethsemane, I was covered. When I turn my will over to the Father, I'm covered. When I pray and intercede for you, I'm covered. Christ was struck with the cat-o'-nine tails so that every time disease and sickness get to me, I'm covered. You're covered. Be set free, in Jesus' name.

God is tearing down denominational barriers so that the children of God can come together and be His Church. For years I've heard that you have to come through a particular church or denomination to make it to heaven. Do you know what I believe? You might go through some organizations and end up somewhere other than heaven. I'm going to put my faith in God. By His stripes I am healed. When I stand and proclaim the gospel, I'm covered.

Look at what Christ did for us:

> He left a world of glory for one of meanness. He left a world of purity for one of crime. He who had created all things was sold for 30 pieces of silver. He who was the source of bliss suffered anguish. He who had worn the royal robes of heaven was clad in the cast-off robe of office. He who had borne the crown of the universe was tormented with mockery (Biblical Illustrator).

Revelation 2:10 says this:

> *Fear none of those things which thou shalt suffer: behold, the devil shall cast some of you into prison, that ye may be tried; and ye shall have tribulation ten days be thou faithful unto death, and I will give thee a crown of life.*

While they mocked Christ, they did not understand that He is the Crown of Glory. You can be crowned with the Crown of Glory by doing one thing-believing. How do you believe? You repent of your sins. You repent of your doubt and confusion. You ask Him to take you, by faith, out of yesterday and into today, walking in total amazement of His glory upon your life.

Even if you can't physically get dressed and drive to a local ministry because of health conditions, you can flip on the television and say, "In the name of Jesus, I'm covered by the blood." It doesn't matter if we're in the church-house or the bathhouse; we're covered.

People are the church, and we become part of His church when we receive Jesus Christ as Lord and Savior. Lord, come in and make me fresh, make me new.

The Word says that when I am saved by the blood of Jesus, as a special gift, I become the righteousness of God. As the righteousness of God, I can stand and bring my sickness, my sin and my disease, and lay it at the altar. If I'm in my home, I can get up and bow down by the couch, or hide my face in the carpet, and say, "Lord, it's just You and me."

God is tearing down the barriers for one reason. He bled seven times that we may live a holy, righteous life, but we, the Church, have missed it. We only celebrate His suffering one day every year, yet He suffered so that we might be delivered every day of our lives.

By His stripes, I'm healed in my mind. By His stripes, I'm going to get that new job. By the blood that was shed at Calvary, when I make intercession for my friends, because I am covered by His blood, something supernatural is going to take place. It is all about learning who you are in Jesus' name. It is all about getting to the place where it doesn't matter what your background is. What matters is that today we have a new, fresh revelation.

A Fresh Revelation

For three years, Christ walked the earth healing every disease. For six hours, He suffered for the sins of mankind. Lord, in honor of Your six hours of suffering, I praise You and exalt You, and I accept You into my life. But then, Lord, for the three years and hundreds of miles You walked the earth to spread the gospel, I honor You. By faith I receive my miracle. At this moment, I don't feel anything supernatural happening, but by faith I know what I am feeling is real. Thank God, I am covered by the blood of Jesus.

Once we receive Jesus Christ as Lord and Savior, what do we do next? It is simple. We start with prayer. "Father, here's my need. I give it to You and turn my will over to Yours. Father, I praise You. I magnify and glorify You, Lord."

Most of us have wondered why we suffer in this life. Perhaps God is going to send someone into your life who has never dealt with what you have already dealt with, and you are going to have a word for that person.

> *Who comforteth us in all our tribulation, that we may be able to comfort them which are in any trouble, by the comfort wherewith we ourselves are comforted of God* (2 Corinthians 1:4).

Because I know I'm covered, I can preach the gospel no matter what is going on in my life. Even when I'm weak, and when my mind is being chiseled, all I have to do is remember, "Hold it, I'm covered." When you, as a believer, are about to have the fight of the year with your spouse because there isn't enough money to pay the bills, take a moment and remember you are covered by the blood of Jesus Christ.

I have an oxymoron, if you will, that teaches something about being covered by the blood. If you get it, it will bring a great truth and revelation to your life. I do not understand how I can reach into my pocket, give away money that I desperately need, and then still pay my bills. If I earn $500 and I pay my tithe, which would be $50, that means I only have $450 left. But I find that I can do more with the $450 than I could with the $500.

Now, I believe this only works if the blood of Jesus has covered you. Somehow, God uses that gift as a way to bless us. It's amazing how the Lord can use something as insignificant as $50 to bless me in return. I don't understand how it works, but that act of obedience and love has amazing results.

It's the same when you find someone who has a need and you give them money, food, or clothing. By the blood of Jesus, that is a form of interceding for someone else. It is important to note that the Bible teaches "It is more blessed to give than to receive" (Acts 20:35).

People protest that churches just want money. I disagree. The Word teaches giving as a form of worship. When you understand the price He paid for you, you won't argue about giving. Sometimes, through the spirit of discernment, the Lord won't say anything about money. He'll simply let us know to give a hug without saying a word. Jesus loves you, and He knows everything that's going on in your life. Understand who you are in Christ, and claim His power and healing, through His blood, for your life.

3

THE CALVARY WALK

There isn't one thing that touches your life for which Christ didn't bleed. We can simply say, "Thank God I am covered by the blood of Jesus Christ. When no one could help me, Jesus was there and He covered me by His blood." When you think about what Christ Jesus did for you and what He means to you, doesn't it do something to you on the inside? It makes me want to celebrate and give Him praise and honor.

I thank God for saving me from a life of sin. I thank God that through my life's struggles, He's with me. I have His promise. I'm not fighting my way alone through life.

When I think about the fact that He agonized because He had me on His mind, it amazes me. Long before the cross, He loved me so much that He cried and suffered that I might have life. We are accustomed to picking up the story at the cross, but so much happened before that. He knew I was going to need someone who would go into a time of agonizing. The Bible teaches us that as He turned His will over to the Father, He agonized to the place that sweat turned to literal drops of blood.

When I turn my will over to the Father, and when 1 begin to intercede for others and begin to care for someone other than myself, I'm covered by the blood. He bore 39 stripes on His back for the 39 major diseases that affect our lives. That means cancer and all forms of disease must go, in Jesus' name. It's covered by the blood. They beat Him, ripped His muscle and meat right off His bones. He suffered because He cared that much for us. He bore the stripes so that I can have my healing, in Jesus' name.

He also wore the crown of thorns. When the pressure gets so heavy, and times get so hard that we feel we are going to lose our minds, we have hope. We can say, "Hold it right there, Satan-you're not taking my mind, because I'm covered by the blood of Jesus."

I believe someone reading this book has a confused mind. I call that mind back in to formulate within the Spirit. When your mind is out there, He says, "Just bring it on back in, child, because everything is okay." For that, He wore the crown of thorns and bled. Thank God, we can have a sound mind in Jesus' name.

The Calvary Walk

As Christ walked up the road the Via Dolorosa, also known as the "way of suffering"-He was on His way to the place called The Skull, or Golgotha, where He was to be crucified. But on the way, He even had to carry His own cross. It's one thing to be beaten and bloodied; however, this just added insult to injury. Can you imagine how He looked and felt? His body was beaten and torn, flesh was hanging from His bones, He'd been slapped, and His face had been spat upon.

I know people don't want gruesome details, but here's the real problem. We wouldn't sin and allow our lives to remain the same if we really understood the pain Jesus bore for us. He suffered more than just a swipe on the back-the flogging literally pulled His skin and meat from His bones. Then, after He suffered all night long, they made Him carry His own cross before they killed Him.

Do you know what that tells me? He carried that cross so that as I carry my load in this life, He will help carry the load. Sometimes the load gets heavy at the workplace or at home; do you ever wish someone would come along and lift the load off of you? On the Via Dolorosa, Jesus lifted the load for you. As He carried the cross, it got so heavy that it weighed Him down; He fell on that winding, rough, rocky road, and skinned His knees. He bled for you and I, so that when we fall under such pressure, we are covered by the blood.

I am covered by the blood not only when I'm losing my mind, but also when there's more on my shoulders than I know what to do with. Or when phone calls come in that I don't understand, things happen in my family, stuff goes on within the realms of the ministry, or the community attacks, and the load gets so heavy that I cry out. It's then that Christ reminds us He bled and died so we may stand.

You may be suffering and you may be under a heavy load, but don't be dismayed. Don't give up. Understand that your knees may be cut and bruised, and you may be bleeding, but He already bled for what you are bleeding over. So, quit bleeding, get on your feet, and understand that He shed His blood for you. When I'm under my load, thank God, I can stand up and say, "Satan, get out of my face, for you forgot that I am covered by the blood of Jesus!" Yes, my cross is heavy. And, yes, sometimes, my cross is a cross of trouble. There are even times I want to lay the cross down. But I will never lay it down, because Jesus carried the cross that I might carry the load He asks me to carry.

Some of you are battling in your mind and battling in your spirit, and some of you simply don't know which way to turn. But understand that you can bring your burden and lay it at the feet of Jesus. He understands the pain. He understands the agony. He knows how many times you have been beaten lower than life.

Life has had its Hay day with me a few times, but because of the path Jesus took, I have hope. At any moment, He could have said, "That's it. It's enough. I quit. I'll not go there. I'm not going to go any further!" But He didn't. He said, "No! No matter how bad it hurts Me-no matter how much suffering, no matter how heavy the cross-I'm going to go all the way for the Father."

Jesus Had a Purpose

Just like little David said years before, when he heard about Goliath, "Is there not a cause?" (1 Samuel 17:29). There's a giant wanting to tear down the Kingdom. There's a giant wanting to make a mockery of the Kingdom! There may be a giant out there who wants to mess up your life. David remembered the bear he conquered with the anointing, and he knew that by the same anointing, this giant would be conquered.

Jesus died for our sins, and if He bled for me, then He bled for you, also, because the Word teaches He is no respecter of persons (Acts 10:34). Just as David conquered the enemy with the anointing, because we are covered by the blood of Jesus we can destroy the enemy that tries to tear us down.

Instead of carrying my load, I'm going to drop it off at the altar, at the feet of Jesus, and say, "Lord, I will no longer carry this load that You've already carried for me." When we are under such agonizing loads, we can thank God He bled. When we simply do not know where to turn, thank the Lord He reminds us He walked that winding road to keep us on the straight and narrow. He paid a price that was too heavy for us to pay. He knew we could not bear the days and torment of life ahead.

I believe He said, "That's okay. For Donald R. Vining, I'm going to pave the way and pay the price. That old Vining is pretty tough, but he's not tough enough for this burden that's coming, so I'm going to go ahead and carry the cross for him. When he gets to the place where he realizes that, as a man, he can only deal with so much, he's going to turn and understand." It was by the blood of Christ Jesus that I am able now to stand and walk freely. What helps me walk and keeps me going? Jesus does, because on that winding road, He made a way. He said in John 14:6 that He is the way, the truth, and the life. On my way to where Jesus is bringing me, He is the one that carries my load.

Jesus bled for the load you are carrying. It's Jesus who enabled you to make it this far in life. Some of you are thinking, "I made it this far, but I just don't think I can go any further." I beg your pardon? He bled 2,000 years ago so you and I could stand under the load. I'll stand today, I'll stand tomorrow, and I'm going to stand next week. I'm going to stand until I hear Him say, "Well done, My good and faithful servant." He walked the road and bled that I might stand in Jesus' name.

You don't have to go through life depressed, frustrated, and hearing everyone tell you that you're nothing. Just stop for a moment and say, "Devil, shut your mouth, and listen to the man of God! He bled that we might stand and do the work that He called us to do. Stick that in your pipe and do whatever you want to do with it." I'm not going to get down because of the pressure and the load of life. Been there. Done that. But then I read in the Book, and He asks, "Don't you know you have been made more than a conqueror?" (Romans 8:37, paraphrased). I picture Christ asking, "Boy, why do you keep on struggling and suffering with the things for which I walked the Via Dolorosa? Boy, go back and remember. I have already suffered so you don't have to."

What is my place? I'll tell you what my place is. It is to stand and celebrate. Jesus paid the price for me-thank God. What is my place? To give joy and honor! If I can't do any thing else than give Him praise and magnify Him for the magnitude of His suffering, that's what I will do. He made it possible for me to have a life of joy,

Calvary's Triumph

Not only did He bleed as He fell down under the load of the cross, but Jesus went all the way to Calvary. You see, the place of the skull, or Calvary-Golgotha-was a place where passersby would come to see who had been crucified. Bible commentaries tell us it's called the place of the skull because it is rounded and looks like a skull. In fact, so many were crucified there that, literally, skulls were lying all around (*Biblical Illustrator*).

Call it Calvary, call it Golgotha, call it whatever you will, but it's the place where the devil and the Lord had a day of reckoning. And, guess Who won? The devil thought he had whipped our Lord and Savior, but what he didn't understand is that he caused Jesus to move into another phase, another arena. Now the devil has to go back and say, "What am I going to do with this? We took His physical life. But look: three days later, He's living. He's alive!" Nobody can take the Lord and Savior out.

At crucifixion, some were tied to the cross and others were nailed. The Word reaches us that Christ was nailed to the cross, and we know that Thomas later asked to see the nail scars:

The other disciples therefore said unto him, We have seen the LORD. But he said unto them, Except I shall see in his hands the print of the nails, and put my finger into the print of the nails, and thrust my hand into his side, I will not believe. And after eight days again his disciples were within, and Thomas with them: then came Jesus, the doors being shut, and stood in the midst, and said, Peace be unto you. Then saith he to Thomas, Reach hither thy finger, and behold my hands; and reach hither thy hand, and thrust it into my side: and be not faithless, but believing. And Thomas answered and said unto him, My LORD and my God (John 20:25-28).

Thomas wanted to see where His Lord and Savior had holes in His body because he wanted to know it was, in fact, his Lord and Savior.

Many of us think Christ was nailed through the palms of His hands. Not so the palm of the hand could not support the weight of the body. Some may argue that the Bible says that's how He was nailed, and it does, but the wrist is a part of the hand. In fact, Scripture even tells us that not a bone was broken in the body of our Lord and Savior (John 19:34). Isn't that amazing?

Think about the pain of a nail being put through that place in the wrist where the most nerves are. Jesus had to be nailed through the wrists because, first of all, they could sup port the weight of His body. Secondly, that was a spot where bone would not be damaged, because the Word prophetically said He would be crucified, but not a bone would be harmed or damaged. Those crucified next to Jesus had their legs broken to hurry their death along, because then they couldn't push up to take a breath, but Jesus' legs remained unbroken. Look up John 19:36 and read it for yourself.

I'll tell you why I believe they nailed Him through the wrists-because, even hanging on the cross when His life was leaving His physical body, He still was saying, "It's okay. This is the way to Calvary. Though they may beat Me, curse Me, spit on Me, and have nailed Me to the cross, be not dismayed, for I am your God!" Those hands had been present throughout the course of time. During the three years of Jesus' ministry on earth, those hands anointed, taught the Word, and communicated authority. Now, those hands were attached to the cross, but His life wasn't over.

Christ knew that even though He was suffering, no men would see the Father unless they first went through the Son. He didn't want them to worry about Him. "You see Me suffering now, but give Me three days, and then you'll see what you're going to get!" (John 2:19, paraphrased.) "I am the way, the truth, and the life" (John 14:6). "Fear not. For I am your God!"

We can boldly tell the devil he'd better look out, because the Savior is not dead in some cave somewhere. He's alive by His Spirit, still pointing the way. Do you know what that tells me? People can persecute me all they want to. They can bring mockery to the house of God and the people of God, but Jesus still tells us to keep our hands up toward Him, even on our deathbeds.

Not only will He help us point the way for a lost and dying world, but when we go under His anointing and lay hands on the sick, our hands represent His hands pointing the way. So, when I say, "In Jesus' name," all I'm saying is, "He is the Way. He is the Truth. He is the Life" (John 14:6). He is the Great Physician-my Hope, my Redeemer, and my Salvation.

Christ Points the Way

Jesus' hands were nailed to the cross to point the way. He is the Way, the Truth, and the Life. I've been asked if I ever struggle. Yes. How do I deal with it? I remember that He is the Way. Do my hands ever grow weary? Yes. But I remember then that He paid the price so I could survive!

He bled when they drove the spikes into his hands. That tells me I can stand because the Bible tells me God is no respecter of persons (Acts 10:34). That means when I have struggles in my life, He bled for my struggles just as much as He did for others. As you and I stand unified in the Spirit, no devil can have his way in our lives.

What is it that makes people struggle with the same struggle, year after year? I have sometimes thought my middle name was "struggle." I have been trying to get "struggle" out of Ray, my middle name, but all I came up with was "reject." I came up with "airhead," and I've even had someone come to my office and call me "yellow."

I may be a lot of things, but I'm not a "yellow belly." I stand on the Almighty Word of God, and I say to you boldly, whatever has touched your life, fear no longer. Maybe physically you can't get out of your home, but you can stretch out your hands and say, "Father, thank You for covering me with the blood of Your Son. Jesus is my Redeemer, my life, and the One I stand upon!" Don't take for granted the blood that was shed when they nailed those hands to the cross.

The Feet of Jesus

Not only did He bleed a fifth time when they nailed His hands to the cross, but also when they nailed His feet. The devil was making one final attempt to stop those feet from spreading the Good News, but if the devil had seen what was coming, he would have been better off leaving the Lord alone.

At that time, only the Lord and a few disciples were doing the Father's work. But when Jesus' feet were nailed, He submitted to the cause of death because He knew the Spirit would be able to do more through many believers lives than He would be able to do as one man. When we accept Christ, we are to be the light that carries the gospel.

Do you want to see God revolutionize your spiritual life? Then get in your prayer closet and start praying. Start fasting. Somebody has to pay the price in prayer. I thank God for the ladies and men of our church who come to pray on Tuesday mornings-sometimes they raise the roof off our church, because prayer is the key. Jesus said it was okay to tie His feet, nail them, and try to stop them. But in three days, He'd be bringing a new revelation.

The Comforter Comes

After He arose, Christ spent time telling more than 500 people to go to Jerusalem, to a place called the "upper room," and stay there, because after Christ conquered death and hell itself, it was the Father's will for Him to go and sit at His Father's right hand. But after He arrived in heaven, He sent the Comforter, the Holy Spirit, to this earth. One way to know if the Comforter is working His will in your life is that you won't be able to sit still.

Jeremiah said it like this: "It's like fire shut up in my bones" (Jeremiah 20:9). In this incidence, Jeremiah had been brought before the city, humiliated, and had suffered all night long. Finally, he said, "Okay, fine if the Lord's going to do this to me, I'm not going to speak another word on His behalf. I'm not going to speak the Lord's name again." After he made up his mind, though, Jeremiah said, "But woe be unto me. I found that it was like fire shut up in my bones!"

Some Sundays, I leave church and want to throw the keys behind me and never look back. But before Monday morning, it's like a fire shut up in my bones. I can't keep silent, because I look and see lives being affected by our ministry. Many more are finding the joy of the Lord than are going stale and molding over.

I have joy because Jesus nailed feet opened the door for the power of the Holy Spirit to come upon my life, so I could spiritually leave the upper room and come to Summerfield and bring the Good News that Jesus is alive. Jesus is what we need. It's the blood of Jesus that we stand upon.

Sometimes on Sunday mornings, I just try to be laid-back "Mr. Polished," but thinking about what it meant when the Lord saved me from a life of sin gets me fired up. When I think about how empty and mundane it was to live without the power of the Holy Ghost in my life, I can't keep it to myself. When I remember that wonderful day at the Ocala church where God so wonderfully filled me with the Baptism of the Holy Ghost, I feel just like Jeremiah.

The Holy Ghost will teach you what man can't teach you (John 14:26). Twelve years ago, I had about 100 kids in my youth group in the tiny little metropolis of Wildwood, Florida. The church folks said, "Boy, you need some education. You can't be a father, a husband, and you can't minister without it." At that time, I was already getting educated-a hands-on education in the School of Hard Knocks. I'm thankful for my formal education, but I'm more thankful that I've learned I have the power of the Holy Ghost to teach me even when man turns his back on me and hates me. Man teaches me how to hate, but by the Holy Ghost, God Almighty teaches me how to love. I want to teach the community that we love mankind like Jesus loved them.

People said, "Preacher, in 10 years you'll not even be able to relate to people." If this dumb old country boy knows anything about math, I know it's been about ten years since I was told that. See, these folks put all their eggs in the basket of education. I thank God for education. I'm about to get a degree. But, before I get educated, until I get educated, and after I get educated, it's still the power of the Holy Ghost that works through these hands and feet and through these lips.

The Holy Ghost was made available because Jesus bled and died a brutal death so we might live. That's the reason I can't stand still. That's the reason I can't hold my peace. That's the reason why, when I feel like crying, I get up and come out fighting, because there is a cause in me. Christ bled in the Garden of Gethsemane. He agonized over me. They beat Him with the cat-o'-nine tails so that, no matter what sickness has hold of me, I'm covered with the blood. They made Him wear a crown of thorns so that, when I felt like I was losing my mind, when I was being mocked, I'd be covered with the blood. They led Him down the Via Dolorosa as a suggestion that, no matter how rocky your road gets, He bled for that road you are walking. When they got Him to Golgotha, they nailed His hands to the cross so that He could point the way. This is the way,

My sons and daughters. And then they nailed those feet.

Sometimes we feel like our feet are nailed to the ground. Do you know what Deuteronomy 11:24 says? "Every place whereon the soles of your feet shall tread shall be yours." I'm claiming wherever God will open the airways for the wonderful gospel. We live in dying, stressful times. The world and the community need to know that Jesus paid the price that we might have life.

Start Living

I encourage you to get to your feet and start living. He bled and died for you. Thank Him that He's your Savior and Lord. Thank Him that He's there with you and that He loves you. Thank Him that He's your healer and that no matter what you face, He is Lord.

I have been criticized and told I shouldn't be so transparent. At times, Christians can be the most hurtful people. At least a sinner will tell you they're coming for you. I'll tell you boldly, I suffer. I have sickness in my body, and there are times I'm depressed. There are times I want to walk out, but before I get out the door, I remember there's a fire that keeps me standing.

I don't speak as someone who's made it to perfection, but guess what? I am on my way to perfection; I am being transformed. No matter what you're experiencing in your life, Jesus bled and died that you might have a better life. That is the reason why I keep living, keep breathing. "Greater is he that is in you, than he that is in the world" (1 John 4:4). I believe that promise. No weapon formed against me shall prosper, says Isaiah 54:17.

Sometimes, when in the midst of a trial you are tempted to walk out, about the time you get to the door, the blood kicks in and says, "Hold it. I said wherever the soles of your feet tread, boy, is yours." Thank God, in all my struggles, He loved me so much that He paid the total price, so I could stand under the load.

My wife has said to me, "You know, sometimes you get under such stress and such pressure that when you come home from the office, all you want to do is lay there like a zombie. You don't even want to pick up a stick out of the yard. Sometimes I think the only joy you have is when you're preaching." I've thought about that a lot. There is great joy in preaching. I can walk into the house of God pain-ridden and troubled in my mind, but before I get out the back door, it's gone! Do you know what I'm striving for? I want the same anointing I feel when I stand in the pulpit and minister to go with me and help me stand every day.

I want to remind you once again. In the book of Jeremiah, we read that when the prophet had been humiliated, hurt, and was obviously exhausted, he responded to his pain by saying he would never speak of the name of God again. He didn't stay that way, however. Jeremiah 20:9 tells the story this way:

> *Then I said, I will not make mention of him, nor speak any more in his name. But his word was in mine heart as a burning fire shut up in my bones, and I was weary with forbearing, and I could not stay.*

It is imperative to understand that even when we feel like giving up, we can remember that the same God who lived within Jeremiah is the same God living within the believer.

There are times in our lives when it seems no one has the answers. In 1 Samuel 30:6, we read about a crisis in David's life:

> *And David was greatly distressed; for the people spake of stoning him, because the soul of all the people was grieved, every man for his sons and for his daughters but David encouraged himself in the LORD his God.*

Thank God we can respond like David did! If you feel there is distance between you and your God, begin to remind yourself of the things God has brought you through, and you will find that the encourager will rise up within you.

4

HIS REASON FOR SUFFERING

Have you ever wondered why Christ chose to suffer? First and foremost, according to Philippians 2:8, He suffered in order that He might obey the Father. "And being found in fashion as a man, he humbled himself, and became obedient unto death, even the death of the cross." Second, He suffered to make the Father known. John 14:9 tells us:

Jesus saith unto him, Have I been so long time with you, and yet hast thou not known me, Philip? He that bath seen me hath seen the Father; and how sayest thou then, Show us the Father?

If you have found Jesus in your heart, then you have seen the Father. If Jesus has touched your life at least one time, you have seen the Father.

Why do we keep seeking for that which we have already seen? It's time to get out of the natural mind and into the supernatural, and say, "Jesus, my Lord, I see You every-where. I see You in the moon. I see You in the sun. I see You in the earth. Lord, everywhere I look, I see Jesus." He suffered to make the Father known.

Third, He suffered that men might be redeemed. Galatians 3:13 says, "Christ hath redeemed us from the curse of the law, being made a curse for us: for it is written, Cursed is every one that hangeth on a tree." Our Lord's suffering was extreme and painful. He suffered in every possible way, in every possible degree. He suffered in His body, He suffered in His soul, He suffered personally, and He suffered relatively. He suffered under the seal of the curse. You see, back in Jesus' time, the Romans only awarded death by crucifixion to criminals. To the Jews, crucifixion was an abomination.

Then again, there are wonderful things to be seen in the manner and circumstances of our Lord's crucifixion. We say, "Oh, He lost His life. He suffered." But look at what we see of the Father through Christ's suffering. The Biblical Illustrator states that we see God withdrawing and, yet, we see God supporting: "The Redeemer, sinking under His sufferings and at the same time rising triumphantly over and above them all."

The last sufferings of Christ are a remarkable accomplishment of the Word of God. Christ fulfilled all the ancient prophecies spoken of in the Old Testament. Throughout the Scriptures, it was prophesied that not a bone in His body would be broken (read John 19:36). All through the Old Testament, it was prophesied that there would be a Savior who would give His life and rise from the dead. All through the Old Testament, we read about the One coming who would be mightier than we are.

In this we see, according to Mark 15:28, that the Word of God is not a lie "And the scripture was fulfilled." He said He would bleed for you-He did. He said He loves you-He does. He said He heals you-He heals you. He said He walks with you-He's with you. He said He would never leave you nor forsake you-you can count on that.

When people tell me they don't "feel" the Lord, I encourage them to let their faith go to work. Then they'll know that without the Lord, they wouldn't be here. If He said it in His Word, you can take it to the bank and draw a little interest on it.

Mark 15:23 reads, "And they gave him to drink wine mingled with myrrh: but he received it not." Compare that to Solomon's words in Proverbs 31:6- "Give strong drink unto him that is ready to perish, and wine unto those that be of heavy hearts." It was common for the most honorable women of Jerusalem to attend criminals at their execution and to give them wine and myrrh to drink before they were put to death (Biblical Illustrator). The drink, say the commentators, was regarded as numbing the nerves and inducing sleep. In His time of suffering, Jesus had an opportunity to receive medication so He would not feel the fullness of the pain.

Jesus was not on an ego trip. He did not receive medication to alleviate His suffering, but rather bore the fullness of the pain we would suffer in this life. He knew His suffering was ordained of the Father.

When you know that the blood covers your life, and you know that God Almighty ordains your life, you'll quit looking for a reason not to suffer. The Bible says Christ suffered. Through different phases of life, we are going to suffer.

The sufferings of Christ were divine-it was a divine calling, not accidental. It isn't just something a man did. He refused the drink so He would not escape the full force of the penalty He had undertaken to endure. In other words, Christ did His job and He did it to the fullest. He was our example.

Christ had many opportunities to walk away from the pain. Anybody can quit. Anybody can make waves. But not just anybody can stand in the footsteps of Christ. Jesus bled and suffered and gave His life that you may stand.

Stand With Purpose

I submit to those of you in church or community leadership, stand up, square your shoulders, be bold, and let your "yea" be "yea" and your "nay" be "nay," When you say it, mean it. Whatever it is that you mean, say it with conviction.

People want to follow a person who has direction. I wouldn't be part of a church that didn't have conviction.

The greatest music program-the greatest preaching, the greatest word-would mean nothing if it didn't spring forth with conviction.

Some of you husbands could take back your home from the devil if you let some conviction fill you. If some of you wives learned to let the man be the man of the house, joy, unity and happiness could come back to the American home. I don't want to offend anyone, but I have to tell you the truth.

Jesus bore stripes. He suffered as an example that in life, we're going to suffer. At times our marriages will go through suffering. Sometimes we're going to suffer with our children. There will be times when we suffer in the workplace, and we're going to suffer in our wallets. But Christ bled, and died, and bore the full brunt of the pain that in the end, we would be found standing. Why? Because we are the Christ of our time.

Anytime you go into the community and are weak-kneed as a believer, you portray Jesus as weak. If I know anything, I know my Lord and Savior was not a weakling. He had an opportunity to numb His nerves, to be put to sleep, but He said no. He stood in God Almighty, His Redeemer, Savior, and Hope. He placed His trust in His Father, the One who stays closer than a brother. "He didn't choose to suffer in order that He might grandly bear it" (Biblical Illustrator). In other words, He didn't have any ego. But because this suffering was ordained of Heaven, He refused to accept any deliverance from man.

How's Your Trust?

The truth of the matter is that we either trust God or we don't. He either heals or He doesn't. He is either my Redeemer or He isn't. If I believe He can heal my big toe with a rotten nail on it, then I believe He can heal my broken heart. And, if I believe He can heal my broken heart, I believe He can heal cancer in my body. And, if I believe He can heal cancer in my body, I believe He can take me out of a life of sin.

God was committed to the greatest suffering of mankind. Your heart would have failed had you walked through the suffering Christ suffered, because His was divine. I'm not going to curse medication or doctors, but I am going to say this-there has to come a time in your life when you trust in yourself and God more than you do man. "Well, Mr. Hotshot, it's easy for you to say, Just drop the medication." No, it isn't. But I know what it is to look out a window and say, "Lord, I'm sick in my body, and my nerves have gone crazy, and Lord, they have me so drugged up I can't even think right to trust You." I know the pain and the agony of saying, "Lord, I really don't believe it is Your will for me to be sick. But if it is Your will, I'm going to be sick without that particular medication, because I'm tired of my mind and my feelings being altered by a bottle." It was a painful moment, but I have accepted the challenge in Malachi 3:10 that says, "Prove me."

God already knows what He's going to do. When we prove Him by the blood of Jesus, He'll come through every time. He will heal you every time. He will bring you peace every time. He will bring you money that you don't have every time. He will bring the husband and wife back together every time.

You can argue with my theology, but you can't argue with my experience. What we need may not always come when we think or how we think it should, but He is an "On-Time" God. He knows what is best for us. The Word says, in John 16:33, "These things I have spoken unto you, that in me ye might have peace. In the world ye shall have tribulation: but be of good cheer; I have overcome the world."

I know who I am in the Lord. I know when the devil comes to shake my home that Jesus bled and died so I could have peace in my home. Single mothers, you can still stand up like the man of the house, because at that moment you are the man of the house. If you don't become the man of the home, the devil's going to take that role, and I wouldn't let the devil come in and wreak havoc in my home. We can say, "Devil, you're a liar. I rebuke you and come against you. I stand saved, sanctified, filled with the Baptism of the Holy Ghost. Devil, you may have won this round, but praise God, victory is mine!"

Christ suffered that I could have victory. I read the end of the Book and we win. I'd love for someone who is in bondage to understand what I am saying. We can say with Job, "though He slay me, I'm going to trust Him." Even though the community comes against me, I still love Him. He is still my Redeemer. Even though I don't have the money I think I should have, money is on the way. He suffered so we could stand. We don't have to live a defeated life. Not long ago, a brother in the Lord hit the nail on the head. We were talking about how people struggle and he said, "You know, the problem is people don't even understand that they can live better lives."

Most people are too concerned with what other people are doing. Instead, get your nose out of Granny's kitchen and into your own business, and understand that Christ's blood covers you. No matter what you are suffering, He already suffered for you. Stop that confounded suffering and stand up, put on the coat of righteousness, and say, "He not only saved me from a life of sin, but I became the righteousness of God. Devil, have a party at my home while I'm gone, but when I get there, you're out of there. Because I understand now I'm covered by the blood of Jesus!"

Digging Deeper

We haven't even scratched the surface of what this truth should mean in our lives. I see people who can have better jobs, better marriages, better families, better children, better ministries, but they don't even realize it. When I see that, I can't just sit back and say, "Praise God, look what we have." Look what we don't have. Look who we don't have.

We ought to be going after the leaders of our communities with prayer and fasting. Get them saved and filled with the Holy Ghost, so that they will start making good, godly decisions for our communities. Instead, we take our little gospel and hoard it, because heaven forbid someone mocks us if we were to speak up. Well mock away, baby. I say, "Devil, look out. Here I come. I'm covered by the blood of Jesus." He is my hope. He is the Wheel in the middle of the wheel, the Lily of the valley, the Bright and Morning Star. He is the great Majestic One, the Great Physician, my Psychiatrist.

The Seventh Time

Let's talk about the seventh time Christ bled. John 19:33-34 says:

47

When they came to Jesus, and saw that he was dead already, they brake not his legs. But one of the soldiers with a spear pierced his side, and forthwith came there out blood and water.

That fulfilled the prophecy that not a bone in His body would be broken. When men hung on the cross, if their legs were not broken, they used them to push themselves up so they could breathe. The soldiers would come along and break the legs of the criminals so that their death would not be prolonged.

Jesus was dead on the cross. The Bible says that when the soldiers came to Him, He had given up the ghost. Gone, dead. He was a dead Christ. Previously, Christ had said, "Destroy this temple, and in three days I will raise it up" (John 2:19). The soldiers feared the words of Christ so much that one of them pierced Him in the side.

Jesus was pierced in His right side, and the metal tip of the lance pierced the membrane around His heart. His bones were not pierced, because the Bible says not a bone was broken. The spear went up underneath His rib cage, and all the way through the heart of Christ.

Have you ever felt like you've had a spear right through the middle of your heart? Have you had your heart crushed? For all those moments in your life, Christ bled for your broken heart. Even in His death moment, He still had the power to resurrect Himself. He still had the power to conquer hell itself. He still had the power to heal my body of a broken heart. They didn't really pierce His side, they pierced His heart.

There are those who say, "Give your heart to Christ and your problems are over." I'm here to refute and rebuke that lie from the pit of hell. The moment you give your life to Christ, the devil comes at you, because he doesn't want you to know you are covered by the blood. He doesn't want you to know you can live a life of peace, joy and happiness. As Christians, we are going to suffer. As Christians, we are going to go through valleys. As believers, we are going to have moments when we hurt.

Do you know why you have suffered disease, but are still living? Think back to what happened to Job and the conversation between

God and Satan. How might I be sure that the devil didn't say to God, "Well, what about old Vining down there in Summerfield? You have placed a hedge around him where I can't touch him." Suppose the Lord God Jehovah said, "Touch all that he has, but you're not going to take his life."

You are living in your diseased moment because God won't let the devil take you out. And you're not going to go out until God gets the fullest glory. So, stop worrying about living and quit worrying about dying. Be glad in who you are. I may be diseased in my body, but I still plead the blood of Jesus upon my home. I am still victorious.

Do you really think people want to be part of Christianity when Christians moan and cry about their problems all the time? Who wants to serve a God like that? Think about it: "Come be a part of our team-we're just barely making it!" Would you want to be a part of that? Not me, baby! I tell my staff, "If you have a bad attitude this week, go home." When people come in, they need to see that the Redeemer lives. They need to see we're about the business of the Lord.

That is why the Bible says we should not forsake "the assembling of ourselves together" (Hebrews 10:25). We are to come together to pray for those who are hurting. When I am not hurting, I can bring strength to others. And when I am hurting, others give their strength to me. When my heart is overwhelmed, I go to where the Rock is represented. When I get depressed. I leave my office and get away from people for a while. If folks dial my number and can't get through, they know to leave me alone for a bit. I go home and fuss, cry, carry on, and kick the trees in the neighborhood. Then I come back and say, "I am a man of God."

Some of you are too busy sharing your crises with those around you when you should be talking to God. The devil doesn't tell his secrets and his plans-why do we tell ours? Why not close our mouths and go to the Rock?

How many times have you read that Jesus is the Rock? He's the Rock on which I stand, the Rock of Ages. In Psalm 61:2, David said, "From the end of the earth will I cry unto thee, when my heart is overwhelmed: lead me to the rock that is higher than I." When your heart is overwhelmed, go to the Rock. The Rock is Jesus. If Christians could only get to the cleft of the Rock, that place where Jesus was pierced.

The cleft of the Rock is right underneath His heart. We are emotional beings, but God knows our hearts.

The heart is sensitive-in fact, the Biblical Illustrator says, "Our heart is so delicate and subtle that a single sound will influence it. It's so sensitive that the glance of an eye can bring joy or fear to the heart."

When I'm hurting, I run to Jesus, and He puts me right under His wings where the Bible says He carries me. He bled the seventh and final time so that when your heart is over-whelmed, you can run to the Rock that is higher than you are. There is safety in the midst of trial, and support when one is almost ready to be swallowed up. "For God hath not given us the spirit of fear; but of power, and of love, and of a sound mind" (2 Timothy 1:7).

Rocks and Honey

Deuteronomy 32:13 reminds us, "He made him ride on the high places of the earth, that he might eat the increase of the fields; and he made him to suck honey out of the rock, and oil out of the flinty rock." Honey comes from the rock. Water comes from the rock. Every believer draws water from it. But the honey may be reserved for those who praise Him who bore our sins in His own body on the tree.

People tell me they've been raised to believe that they don't have to praise Him. I believe that if you're not going to praise Him, you're not going to get any honey. Syrup is good on a biscuit, but there's nothing like honey. What is the honey? It is the joy, the peace, the harmony, the prosperity, and the walk of encouragement. It shows itself in a walk with God that people want to follow, in Jesus' name. You can't have the honey if you don't worship Him.

Let's be bold. Say, "Lord, I need some honey!" We praise Him, because we have run to the cleft of the Rock. Even when I'm hurting,

I praise Him. Even when I'm lonely, I praise Him. Even when I don't understand, I praise Him. Even when things aren't going the way I think they should go, I praise Him. As I praise Him, I receive honey.

Deuteronomy 32:13 also says not only do you get honey from the rock, oil comes from the flinty rock. A flint rock is very hard, and if you hit it just right, it will throw a spark. Power, Anointing, Holy Ghost, Word, Security, Healing.

I'm going to praise the Lord-no matter what. Have you ever felt like you were walking the rough, rugged, rocky Via Dolorosa, where everywhere you turned, somebody was slapping your face? I'll be honest with you. Recently I faced so many different challenges in the office, on the road, and at home-that I began to wonder if anything more could go wrong.

Every time the phone rang, somebody had something to say. When I got out of my automobile, somebody chased me down with something else to say. When I got home, there was a message about something else that had gone wrong. Someone asked how I could go through all that, and still go to church and preach with joy and happiness. I'll tell you how: I began to give Him praise and I received honey, and in the midst of the honey-gathering time, I received oil-oil comes from the flint rock when I go through those tough times. That's why I can stand. That's the reason I can smile.

He bled for you seven times, that you might live a happy and joyful life. We go through difficult times to show us how to get to the honey. The children of Israel were in the desert for 40 years, but they were promised the land of milk and honey. I'm going to buy 10 or 15 gallons of honey and, when people ask what that is, I'm going to say, "That's Jesus."

One Friday afternoon, my wife asked, "What else could go wrong?" Then came Saturday, and she said, "Well, there's another chapter to the story that I need to tell you." At times like that, in the flesh, you just feel like getting up and walking out. But then the honey of the Spirit begins to flow and soothe all those hurt places. As that honey comes, I begin to plainly see that all I need to do is go to the Rock-Jesus Christ, my Lord and Savior.

I don't care where you're living, or what you're walking through, or what your religious background is. Because Christ was pierced through the side to get to His heart, we can begin to give Him praise and give Him all our hurts. Isaiah 40:31 says we shall "mount up with wings as eagles… shall run, and not be weary, and [we] shall walk, and not faint," because we know something the world doesn't know. When we're in turmoil, walking through the valley of the shadow of death, the more we praise Him, the more that sweet honey comes. And as we're praising Him and walking through that valley, we also go to the flint rock, and oil comes.

Oil is an insignia of the anointing. Lord, I am walking through a valley that is bigger than I am, but I'm going to praise You, Father, that the anointing would be manifested in my life. I get down sometimes, but the oil of the Spirit keeps me up.

The seventh and final time Jesus bled, they pierced Him in the side to create the cleft. The damage they did to His side the cleft in the Rock-that is my place of refuge.

> The flinty rock represents a stronger image of rockiness. When we are brought into wild and rough places, it is then that we are able to find even richer provisions. Honey is for tough times. Oil is for the most rugged times (*Biblical Illustrator*).

He bled that we might live. He bled that understanding might come. The more we praise Him, the more the anointing is manifest upon our lives; the more the anointing has free reign, the freer we are in giving to His cause. So, money is not even the issue-it is getting you in the right contact with the Rock.

Watch Your Words

When you say negative things, even out of innocence, it is like taking a spear and mutilating the person with whom you are speaking. I built a beautiful home in Belleview, because my wife and I have worked side by side for 45 years so that we could have a nice home. We feel we can't even have a house-warming party, because someone's going to get mad and jealous, and be ugly, and say mean, hurtful things. That is no different than taking a spear and piercing our hearts.

If I see someone prosper and move ahead in life, and I allow myself to say hurtful things, even out of innocence, it's going to get back to that person. When it does, it's going to rip his or her heart out. I thank God that we can hide in the cleft of the Rock.

If someone is my friend to my face, then let him be my friend behind me, too. You may say something out of innocence, but the person sitting at the next table doesn't know that. They hear something negative, and they may not even give your ministry a chance. Every Sunday morning and Sunday evening, people in your community are watching. Though we may say something out of innocence, it pierces the heart of the one who does not understand.

It is obvious there Is an onslaught. The enemy hates your guts, and he wants to mess up your head, but I have good news. Committing your will to God is an indication that you want God more than you want whatever is out there. In Him, I'm coming to the cleft of the Rock, and in Him I will stand; I do stand.

We're going to serve notice on the devil that he has pushed us as far as he's going to push us. He's had his fun, but now I refuse to allow a sour mouth to get me off base with the cleft of the Rock. Christ is my hope, my security, and my Redeemer. As you begin to give the Lord praise, the honey of the Spirit will come.

Father, You see hearts that feel they have been pierced, wounded, even murdered. But God, You are the Rock, the Wheel in the middle of the wheel, our Redeemer. When we are troubled, we can run to the cleft of the Rock.

Father, we lift up those who have had their hearts ripped out, and those facing the doctor's report. We pray for the friend who has turned on a friend, the husbands and wives who have walked out on their families, the children that are troubled. Lord, pour out honey from the Rock of Your Spirit on us. For those who are walking through a stony place, let the oil of Your Spirit come forth to give them direction.

Lord, in some small way, I praise You. I thank You that my heart is bigger than circumstances. I thank You, Lord, that as Your children, we can find hope and restoration, even when we are troubled.

Friend, take your hurt and offer it up to the Lord. The seventh and final time the Master bled was for those times in which you are now suffering. Receive the oil of the Spirit. Receive His love and His fresh touch. Receive Him this day.

5

THE MYSTERY OF BLOOD AND WATER

We know that Christ bled seven different times, and we know that He gave His life. No matter what is going on in your life, Jesus Christ bled for you. He agonized long before the cross, and He agonized all the way through the process of the cross. I find it very interesting that when they pierced Jesus in the side, the Bible says blood and water poured out of His body into the earth. I want to know where this blood and water went.

We know by the Scripture that there are two types of water: one is spiritual and the other natural (Psalm 51:2; Numbers 20:11), We know that the spiritual part of the water is simply the anointing, it's a part of the Holy Spirit. I like to look at it this way. We know that fire, wind, and water have to do with the Holy Spirit. I like to say, "God the Father-Fire, the Holy Spirit-Wind," for He breathed on us by His Spirit. And the water relates to Christ.

Christ shed blood. His anointing-the anointing that flowed out of His body into the earth-has a significant impact all around the world. The prophet Jeremiah, 430 years before Christ gave His life, was told to go and buy a piece of land, take the deed, place it in a jar and preserve it, hold it. He was told to hide it, if you will. He did not fully understand what God was doing, but the land Jeremiah purchased happened to be the land beneath Golgotha.

Hebrews 9:11-14 says:

But Christ being come an high priest of good things to come, by a greater and more perfect tabernacle, not made with hands, that is to say, not of this building; Neither by the blood of goats and calves, but by his own blood he entered in once into the holy place, having obtained eternal redemption for us. For if the blood of bulls and of goats, and the ashes of an heifer sprinkling the unclean, sanctifieth to the purifying of the flesh: How much more shall the blood of Christ, who through the eternal Spirit offered himself without spot to God, purge your conscience from dead works to serve the living God?

If the blood of the Messiah didn't have to be put on the Mercy Seat in the true sanctuary, why does Scripture talk like this? The Bible teaches us that when Christ gave His life, the earth split open and Jesus' blood flowed into the opening of the earth where the Mercy Seat of God was (Matthew 27:51). The veil in the temple that separated man from God was torn in two. The blood flowed beneath Golgotha to this hidden place, this place known as the place of the Ark of the Covenant. It was a secret place. In the same way, today, we can enter into the secret place where we have a personal relationship with the Lord Jesus Christ.

We know that the Mercy Seat of God could not be what it is without the shedding of the blood of Jesus Christ.

Hebrews 9:15-17 puts it this way:

And for this cause he is the mediator of the new testament, that by means of death, for the redemption of the transgressions that were under the first testament, they which are called might receive the promise of eternal inheritance. For where a testament is, there must also of necessity be the death of the testator. For a testament is of force after men are dead: otherwise it is of no strength at all while the testator liveth.

We know that from Gethsemane all the way to the shedding of the blood on the cross, to the blood pouring out of Christ's body, it flowed and soaked into the earth to cover the Mercy Seat. The Mercy Seat was needed because the moment it was covered with the blood, the veil was rent. There was no other place that the crucifixion and the Ark of the Covenant could ever be in order for the Scriptures to be true.

In other words, that wall or veil separated me from God yesterday, but today there is no more separation. Today, I'm covered by the blood of Jesus. Yesterday, you could speak negatively about me and tell me I wasn't going to make it, but today, I know the veil was rent so that I could enter into the Holy of Holies. I can come to that place and worship the King of kings and Lord of lords. I can celebrate that He shed His blood and agonized for me, so that His blood, through the Mercy Seat, would cover me. No matter what I suffer in this life, I am covered. Thank God, I am covered by the blood of Jesus.

We know that the blood of Christ covered the Mercy Seat. That is why we can preach mercy and direct others to the Mercy Seat. All we need to do is go to the Throne Room. We need to tap into what Christ, with His life, prepared for us.

I'm so glad I don't have to look at an idol. I bow down and worship Christ. I thank God I can stand and say, "My God, I worship and magnify You. I can't see You with my natural eye, but in my spirit, I see You holding me in the palm of Your hand." Do you know what that tells me? When I feel dead within myself, His hand lets me feel life. Jeremiah says it's like fire shut up in his bones. I want people to under-stand the blood and water that flowed out of Christ's body can make those who are dead, alive again.

You've seen some of those people who worship actively-don't make fun of them-it's a result of the hand of Almighty God. We don't all worship the same way, because the Spirit affects each one of us differently. Otherwise, we would all just be a bunch of robots. Thank God, the Mercy Seat was covered by the blood that we might preach grace and mercy.

What About the Water?

When someone chooses to be an organ donor, certain internal organs will be donated after that person's death to give others life. While the soldiers viewed Christ dead on the cross-for He had given up the ghost, He was a dead man-His internal organs still shed life. Not just life, but the ultimate life.

You see, the enemy thought, "I've conquered. We killed Him. He could save man, but He couldn't save himself. Mission accomplished!" But what the soldiers did not under-stand is that while they counted the flesh dead, the spirit lived on. There's that blood and water. Man looked at Him and said, "He's dead," but the Spirit of God lived on.

Some of you may look dead on the outside, but thanks to the hand of God, through the blood of Jesus Christ, there is life. Not just life, but life more abundantly. "But Pastor, the doctor said I was going to die!" Yep. We're all going to die in the flesh some day. But let me tell you, to die is to gain. To die simply means that I step out of this life and its turmoil, and into the glorious resurrection of Jesus Christ our Lord and Savior.

That is why we don't mourn those who die in the Lord; we celebrate. I love a funeral where I can say we're having a celebration, not mourning a death. Some of you need the peace of mind and heart that comes from knowing that if your relatives and friends leave this life knowing Jesus Christ as Lord and Savior, they are walking with Jesus in Heaven. Today, they are dangling their feet in the River of Life. Today, they know no sickness, no pain, no suffering, and no sorrow. In fact, they are up there walking on streets of gold. It matters not what I gain in this life, because when I get on the other side, as the old timers would say, "I got myself a mansion waiting on me!" It's because of the Mercy Seat.

We know that there are references, all through the Scriptures, to natural water. In Exodus 17:6, it's for drinking. In Psalm 51:2, it's for cleansing "Wash me thoroughly from my iniquities and cleanse me from my sin." That's a spiritual cleansing.

Water is for washing. In Leviticus 14:8, it's for ritual cleansing, and in Genesis 18:4, it's for washing feet. In Psalm 26:6, it's for washing hands. There were those in the Word who carried the water, in 1 Samuel 9:11. In Revelation 22:1, it is known as the Water of Life: "And he shewed me a pure river of water of life, clear as crystal, proceeding out of the throne of God and of the Lamb." Do you realize that Jesus Christ, our Lord and Savior, is the Lamb? They thought He was dead, but His life was just beginning to have an impact the world had never known. That is why we can stand and say, "I'm saved. The Spirit of Sanctification is working in my life. It's a daily process and I am full of the Holy Ghost, which means I am empowered by the River of Life."

When I bring the Word, you are not hearing a man, but you're hearing the River of Living Water spring forth. I wouldn't sit in a house of worship where I couldn't experience the River of Living Water. I'm telling you the River of Living Water can do more than programs; it can do more than money; it can do more than you and I can do collectively. We must get in the Spirit and say, "Father, I want to flow in the Spirit!" I'm going to shut my mouth and let the Spirit of God lead me and speak to me. While my friends and neighbors are telling me it's over and it won't work, the Spirit of God says, "Yep! You're right. That's what man says, but hear the voice of the Most High God."

Jesus Christ bled and died so that I would have salvation in my life, and then water flowed out of His body so that the River of Life may flow freely in my life. If you'd like to get a revival going in the midst of your family, then let it start within you first. God is waiting on you to shout. He's waiting on you to say, "Look what He's done in my life. Look how He saved and sanctified me!"

He took this old boy, bankrupt and full of leukemia, fighting a nervous condition, and turned my life around. It is because of the blood and the anointing through the water that flowed out of Christ's body that I have life in my veins.

Follow the River

A song out there in the world says something like, "I dropped a bomb on you, baby." I'm going to drop a bomb on you, and implode your spirit. You're going to want to turn the television off and give God praise all day long. Some of you have been thinking that salvation was all there was to it, but when you become empowered by the Spirit of the Anointing of the Most High God-when you have that upper-room experience-you'll do more than just say, "Well, that was another great service."

We know that water, an insignia of the anointing, flowed out of Jesus' body into the earth, but where did it go? In Mark 15:24, it says that Christ was crucified. John 19:34 tells us "One of the soldiers with a spear pierced his side, and forthwith came there out blood and water," into the earth. After He rose from the dead, He told some five hundred to "Tarry ye in the city of Jerusalem, until ye be endued with power from on high" (Luke 24:49).

The people were told to tarry in the upper room, but today we are to tarry in the house of God. When people come into a church and receive miracles, and are delivered from a life of sin, it is nothing more than an upper-room experience. Those experiences can only come when we spiritually visit the house of God. God's house is not a building. God's house is what you perceive it to be on the inside. If we can get out of our natural way of thinking and get into the spiritual part of God, we would know that the Holy Spirit is there every day.

When I made reservations the other night and said there were three of us, the hostess looked at me like I was funny. I said, "It's my wife and I, and the Holy Ghost." The house of God goes wherever I go. Understand that you don't go to church to receive the house, but you bring the house with you that the house would be enlivened. That's why some of you won't pray at home or read the Word-you leave it all up to the man of God. But what if the man of God walks out? What if Mom and Daddy turn and walk away? What if the music director doesn't show up? You need to have your own personal relationship with Christ, no matter what anybody else says or does.

People will meet me at the back door on Sunday mornings and say, "Pastor, that's the greatest message I ever did hear." But I could stand and preach the same Word, with no one there, and I'd meet myself at the back door and say, "Man of God, that was the greatest Word I think I have ever experienced." We are not subject to man's way and man's thinking; it's the Spirit of God that matters.

Blood and water poured into the earth. We know that Acts 2 says that Pentecost the fire, wind, and water-came. We know that Golgotha was known as the "place of the skull." On the outside, it appeared to be a dead place, but on the inside, man couldn't touch what God was doing. Man had an external plan; God had an internal plan.

That's why Jesus said it was okay to tear down His house-His body-because "I will destroy this temple that is made with hands, and within three days I will build another made without hands" (Mark 14:58). He let them beat and disfigure Him, bloody His back, tear out His beard, crush thorns into His skull, spit in His face, curse Him, and crucify Him. He knew that in three days, He would rise again.

Some of you need to understand you are living in the third day of God, and it's resurrection time. You've been living a dead, mundane Christian life, and it's time to let the Spirit of God come alive. It's time to say, "I started my day one way, but I'm going to bed another way, because the Spirit of God is reviving me."

Ezekiel's Vision

The Bible records in chapter 47 of the book of Ezekiel how the prophet and his guide followed the stream as it ran down from the Holy Mountain. The prophet walked 1,000 cubits (that's 1,500 feet), and then he stepped into the water. It says, behold, the waters were ankle deep. He got out of the water and walked another 1,000 cubits, or another 1,500 feet, for a total of 3,000 feet. He stepped in the water and the water was knee deep. And then he got out of the water and trucked on down another 1,000 cubits, which is a total of 4,500 ft.

Now, as a frame of reference, 1,500 feet is just over a quarter mile, 3,000 feet is just under a half a mile, and 4,500 feet is just under a mile. The Bible says that he walked 4,000 cubits, or another 1,500 feet, which brings it to 6,000 feet, which was just under a mile and a quarter. At that point, the Scripture says the waters were deep enough to swim in.

Here's what intrigues me about this: the upper room had to be something spectacular. What greater time for the out-pouring of the Spirit than on the Day of Pentecost, since there were thousands from all over the world in Jerusalem? It was feast time. While they were celebrating the feast, they didn't know there was a feast taking place on the inside.

Jesus told some 500 to go to the upper room, but only 120 showed up, which is par for the course, right? You tell your child to pull the weeds from around four plants, and he'll get three and forget the fourth. You ask someone to go do something, they'll get it half-done and forget about it. But Christ knew they would never make it without the filling of the Holy Ghost, whom He called "the Comforter." We need the Comforter. People don't come to hear me preach on Sundays, they come to hear the Word of Almighty God. I know that's true; otherwise, I could say one thing that would tick them off, and they would get up and walk out. We can't walk out on what the Spirit of God is saying.

Understand that Christianity is not a thing with man, but it's a relationship with God. God said if we didn't praise Him, "I tell you that... the stones would immediately cry out" (Luke 19:40). I'm not saying I'm holy, only that I'm better than I was when I was a sinner. I'm not perfect, either. I've got a ways to go, but I'm better today than I was yesterday.

The River of Life you are experiencing is same River of Life that I'm experiencing. Sometimes I can't wait for Sunday morning and Sunday night, so I can be revived in the Spirit. Sometimes when I get to church, I know how I am in the natural, and it's not very good. But when the Spirit comes on the man, he's like a man from another planet. It's the Spirit and the anointing and the power of the Holy Ghost. We need the Holy Ghost in our lives.

Some folks are afraid of the Holy Ghost. They've been taught that if they receive Him, they're going to have to do something they don't want to do. Wrong. The Holy Ghost is a perfect gentleman, and won't cause you to do something that will embarrass you. If you were embarrassed the last time you shouted, it wasn't God. When God Almighty comes on you, you will have no fear of what man thinks. In fact, others will be intrigued. They will be picked up in the Spirit, because they see the spirit man being fed by the Spirit God. "God is a Spirit: and they that worship him must worship him in spirit and in truth" (John 4:24).

Does it bother me when someone gets up and dances a little jig? No. I know that my spirit bears witness with his or her spirit. There have been times, though, when someone got up who wasn't in the Spirit. How did I know? It grieved my soul.

It is time to clean up the house of God so there can be pure, unadulterated worship. Like the upper-room experience, when we all get in one mind and in one accord, healing is coming to the house of the Lord. The prophet walked three thousand cubits, and it was waist deep. By the time he'd walked four thousand cubits, or just under a mile and a quarter, the Bible says "It was a river that [he] could not pass over: for the waters were risen, waters to swim in, a river that could not be passed over" (Ezekiel 47:5). In other words, it was a river no one could cross.

Nobody is going to glory without crossing the river. And you can't cross the river without the Spirit of God. Some of you have been tap dancing around in ankle-deep water, but I encourage you to come on downstream, where the water is deep enough to swim in. When the waters are deep enough to swim, I am no longer in control. When it is ankle-deep, I can get in or get out. When it is knee-deep, I can get in or get out. When it is waist-deep, I can't run out, but I can still get out. When it is deep enough to swim in, God Almighty alone is in control.

The further the water flows, the deeper it goes. Sounds just like that church talked about in Acts 2 that began in the upper room. It started out as a little trickle, but the Bible says water flowed from the threshold of the house of God (Ezekiel 47:1).

That tells me something had to happen back up the road. In just under a mile and a quarter, the water was deep enough to swim in. Do the math. Go to the place called Golgotha, where Jesus gave His life. From the place of the cross to the upper room (Acts 1:4) is just under a mile and a quarter. Water flowed out of Jesus' body, into the earth, and stayed underground, so when you got there and got your mind right, it would spring up a well of living water.

He is not dead. He is alive by His Spirit. If you feel shallow, come on with me, because God is about to bring you knee-deep, then waist-deep, then chest deep, and then all the way under. Tell the Lord you want to go all the way under, so that it is no longer you, but Christ and Him only. Calvary-the "place of the skull," death as far as the eye could see. Then the earth cracked, and blood flowed, and covered the Mercy Seat. We assume the water has dried up and gone, but it hasn't. Whether or not there is a manifestation of the Spirit, the Spirit of God lives on.

The Upper-Room Experience

Those in the upper room were of one mind and of one accord. They were all worshiping the same God, at the same time, with the same purpose. Praise Him until worship comes, and worship until the glory comes. Then stand and behold the mighty manifestation of the power of the Holy Ghost.

We need to get out of the natural way of thinking, and get rid of our doubting-Thomas attitudes. We need to be able to say we believe in what we have never seen with the natural eye. That means the closer I get to the upper room, the more the power of God comes.

At the time of Pentecost, people in Jerusalem were astonished when they heard the gospel preached in their own language. When God comes, you can't explain all the different ways in which He touches people's lives. In fact, three thousand joined the Jerusalem church in one day. We are talking about the anointing and the church.

God's Long-Term Plan

Because God can see past, present, and future all at once, His perspective on events is far different than ours, What happens to you today may not make sense to you, but God sees the whole picture. He knows the whole plan. Over 400 years before Christ gave His life, Jeremiah purchased a piece of land, took the deed, and hid it in a jar (Jeremiah 32). This was a representation of the Ark of the Covenant. Four-hundred and thirty years later, Christ suffered and died. The natural-thinking man counted Him out. In His death, they took one last jab at Him. They pierced His heart, and blood and water ran to the Mercy Seat.

From the Mercy Seat, water flowed out of the body of Christ into the earth. From Calvary, it flowed to the upper room, which is the house of God. From God's house, it flowed to the local church. From the local church, it flowed to the community, and from the community to the neighborhood.

God had it all worked out. God gave us the power and the anointing not by who we are, but by what we are in the Spirit. And God is enlivening your spirit, so that when you get home from church, you are going to have to say to your neighbor, "You have got to go with me just one time." You'll describe how you have found a place where the River of Living Water flows. You were hurting, depressed, eaten up with cancer, but thank God, that cancer dried up in one of those old-time Pentecostal meetings. It is nothing more than the upper-room experience in modern times.

We need the power and the anointing of the Holy Ghost, the River of Living Water. It amazes me when folks come up to me after a service and ask if I've been preaching at them. They tell me they have a financial dilemma, or a spouse is leaving, or they were at the emergency room at three in the morning with their baby. I don't have to be there, because when we are full of the power of the Holy Ghost, we have no need for a man to teach us (read 1 Corinthians 2:13). When I bring forth the word of God, He knows who will be in the services. He knows what needs to be said to reach the hearts of men and women.

I want to see God change people's lives just like He changed my own. I know how low I have been in my own life, and I have seen what Jesus did for me. I have read in the Bible that He was no respecter of persons (Acts 10:34). That means no matter what I walked through, if He brought me out of it, He will bring you out of it.

Some of you have walked through battles and conquered ground I have yet to discover. But I'll know that when I get to the valley, you've already walked through it, because I've got the testimony in my spirit. And because you have already experienced what I am going through, God can use you to help me. Therefore, it doesn't matter if I go bankrupt, lose my family and my position, or have to sell fertilizer to feed my family. It doesn't matter, because God made a way for the church to live-all the way from Calvary.

We are the church. God doesn't want us to keep quiet with the revelation that He came to feed us. He shed His blood from Gethsemane, all the way down the Via Dolorosa, until they hung Him on the cross and He said, "It is finished." Man thought it was over, except for one. He had just a little bit of the Spirit of God, because he went back to the chief priest and said, "You know that man who is dead? He said something about destroying that body and recovering it in three days. Do you think we should make sure some of his family doesn't go take the body?" The chief priest told him to go guard the tomb.

The devil has come to set up a host of his angels, not heavenly angels, around you (read Ephesians 6:12). This is why we don't fight in the natural. You mess against me, fine. I'm not going to punch you in the nose; I'm going to go to my prayer chamber, and I guarantee that God will move you out of my way.

We spend too much time fighting people. Go to your prayer chamber instead. It is time to stop preaching denominations, to stop living in bondage, and to tear down the walls and say, "We are the body of Christ, and that is all that matters to Him." Red, yellow, black, and white-we are precious in His sight.

There is a deeper measure of His Spirit yet to be experienced. Wouldn't it be a mundane life if we had already experienced all of

God? "O the depth of the riches both of the wisdom and knowledge of God! How unsearchable are his judgments, and his ways past finding out!" (Romans 11:33). If God showed us more of Himself right now, our heads would explode off our shoulders.

It is the Mercy Seat, through the anointing of God, that will touch your life. The Old Testament is the account of a nation. The New Testament is our guide. Thank God that Pentecost happened in the New Testament. We can't see the Son, Jesus Christ, unless it is by the Spirit. God wants to touch our souls, and if we allow the Holy Spirit to do that, the Spirit of God will take care of all those external needs as well. The Scripture tells us to "Seek ye the kingdom of God" (Luke 12:31); "But seek ye first the kingdom of God, and his righteousness; and all these things shall be added unto you" (Matthew 6:33). The word "seek" means to worship. As we give worship to Him, He will bring revelation to us, and with that, He will meet every need.

BIBLIOGRAPHY

Barbet, Pierre. *A Doctor at Calvary*. Garden City, New York: Image Books Edition, a Division of Doubleday & Co., Inc., 1963.

Exell, Joseph S. *The Biblical Illustrator.* Grand Rapids, Michigan: Baker Book House, 1973.

Holman Bible Dictionary. Nashville, Tennessee: Holman Bible Publishers, 1991.

Nelson's New Illustrated Bible Dictionary. Thomas Nelson Publishers, 1996.

Thompson Chain Reference Bible, The. Indianapolis, Indiana: B.B. Kirkbride Bible Company, Inc., 1988.

Webster's Universal Dictionary. New York: The World Syndicate Publishing Co., 1936.

www.ingramcontent.com/pod-product-compliance
Lightning Source LLC
Chambersburg PA
CBHW051236120626
46547CB00013B/1668